Scars & Strength

A LIFE OF PAIN, POWER, AND PURPOSE

Jaitrali

Edited by Abha Srivastava

notionpress.com

INDIA · SINGAPORE · MALAYSIA

ISBN

Hardcase 979-8-89929-921-6
Paperback 979-8-89929-675-8

Dedication

To my childhood sweetheart—my husband—you have been my anchor in every storm, my unwavering strength when I had none left to give. Through every battle, every heartbreak, and every moment I wanted to surrender, you held me together. This book is as much yours as it is mine.

To my two precious children, my greatest gifts in this life—you are my reason to keep fighting. Your love, laughter, and unwavering belief in me has been a ray of sunshine in my darkest moments. Thank you for making me a mother.

To my mother, whose love knows no bounds—you have been my silent warrior, holding me up even when I couldn't stand. Your sacrifices, your prayers, and your endless faith in me has been the foundation of my strength.

To my family, that has stood by me with love, patience, and understanding—you have given me the courage to rise, again and again.

This book is for you, because without you, I wouldn't have had the power to write it.

CONTENTS

• • •

ACKNOWLEDGEMENTS

No journey is ever walked alone and mine has been shaped by the unwavering support, kindness and guidance of so many. This book would not have been possible without each of you.

To my doctors and healthcare providers—thank you for your relentless efforts, your patience and for helping me navigate the uncharted waters of autoimmune illnesses. You have not only treated me but have also given me the knowledge and strength to keep fighting.

To my mentors and friends—your encouragement, your belief in me and your constant reminders of my worth have carried me through the moments I doubted myself the most. Thank you for standing beside me, for listening, and for never letting me forget who I am beyond my struggles.

To the warriors I have met along this journey—those who live with invisible battles, yet wake up every day and choose to keep going—you inspire me more than words can say. Your strength, your resilience, and your shared stories have given me purpose. This book is, in many ways, for you.

To my past colleagues and the digital marketing world—thank you for the years of learning, the challenges that shaped me, and the foundation that allowed me to navigate towards my true calling. My transition from Digital to Psychotherapy was not an easy one, but every step was guided by the lessons I carried from my career.

To my clients and the people who trust me with their pain—you have given me more than I could ever give you. Thank you for allowing me into your lives, for teaching me the depths of human resilience, and for proving that healing is always possible, even when the journey feels impossible.

To faith, the unseen force that carried me through when I had no strength left of my own—thank you for reminding me that even in darkness, there is light.

And lastly, to every person reading this book—you are part of this journey now. May these words bring you comfort, validation, and the knowledge that no matter how hard the battle, you are never alone.

Preface

Scars and Strength: A Life of Pain, Power, and Purpose

This isn't just a book. It's a heartbeat. A lived truth. A battle cry.

Scars and Strength is the deeply personal story of a woman who's been through more than most can imagine—from losing her father as a child, being shuffled between homes, surviving abuse, to living every day with Multiple Sclerosis, Crohn's, psychosomatic asthma, and physical paralysis. But this isn't just about what broke her—it's about how she kept rising.

She was told she wouldn't walk again. She did.

She was told she wouldn't live long. She's still here—fiercely, honestly, imperfectly alive.

This book weaves together her memories, heartbreaks, burn injuries, and hospital stays with the wisdom she's gained as a psychotherapist. It's for anyone who's ever felt like giving up. For those carrying invisible battles. For those longing to feel understood.

Every chapter holds space—for pain, for healing, and for the messy, beautiful in-between.

It's not a polished story. It's a real one.

Because real is what heals.

A Gentle Request Before You Turn the Page

As you journey through Scars and Strength, you'll notice that each chapter ends with carefully crafted reflection exercises and journaling prompts. These aren't just add-ons. They are the heart of your healing experience.

My earnest request to you, dear reader, is this: Please don't skip them.

I encourage you—whether you're reading this on Kindle, listening on Audible, or holding the printed pages in your hands—to keep a notebook or a simple sheet of paper nearby. A pen. A quiet moment. That's all you need.

Because this isn't just a book to read. It's a mirror.

The journaling prompts are designed to slow you down, help you pause, and gently turn inward. They'll guide you to unpack your own wounds, rewrite old narratives, and reclaim your strength—not just by understanding my story, but by finding your own within it.

Without that deeper engagement, this book may remain just words. But with reflection and honesty, it becomes a companion. A conversation. A path.

So please—feel every chapter, and then write with it. Let your scars speak back.

• • •

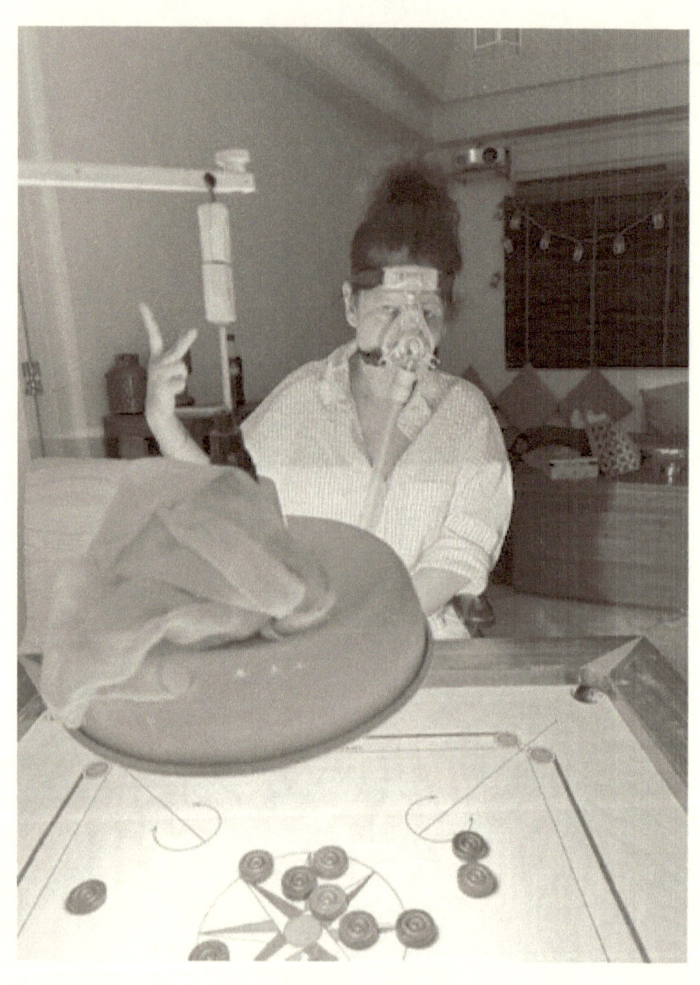

A WARRIORS JOURNEY

I never set out to write a book (till my therapist insisted I do). In fact, for most of my life, I simply focused on surviving.

From childhood, I learned that life was a battlefield, and if I wanted to make it through, I had to be a fighter. I didn't get the luxury of an easy childhood or a smooth path forward. Every step I took was met with resistance—circumstances that tried to break me, obstacles that tried to hold me back—But I kept walking. I kept pushing.

Then, life drew me into battles that I was utterly unprepared for.

Multiple Sclerosis.

Crohn's Disease.

Psychosomatic Asthma.

My body became both the battlefield and the enemy. For a long time, I lived in denial, choosing ignorance over fear. But illness doesn't wait for you to be ready. It forces you into the fight, whether you want it or not.

For years, I was known for my successful career in digital marketing. But behind the success was a woman slowly coming apart. And when life collapsed in a matter of moments, when my body refused to cooperate and I was forced to retire far earlier than I had ever planned, I had to redefine everything.

Who was I without my work?

Without my independence?

Without my strength?

This book is the answer to that question.

Scars and Strength is not just my story—it's a testament to the resilience of the human spirit. It is about what it means to fight battles, not just with the world but within yourself. It is about the scars seared on us, not as symbols of defeat but as proof that we have survived.

I am writing this book because I don't want to leave this world without articulating my truth. My desire is to create awareness about autoimmune disorders, to break the silence around chronic illnesses and to remind every person fighting an invisible battle that they are not alone. I want to share the lessons that pain has taught me, the victories that felt impossible and the truth that even in the darkest moments, there is still light.

If you are reading this, I want you to know: No matter what life has thrown at you, you are stronger than you think. You are more resilient than you realise. And no matter how many scars mark you, they do not define your defeat—they define your survival.

This is my story. But in many ways, it is yours too.

The War Within: A Journey of Pain, Power and Purpose

There's a category of illness that defies logic, a silent war that rages beneath the skin—one with no known cause and no cure. Autoimmune disorders. Over 80 different conditions fall under this cruel umbrella, each one turning the body against itself, each one an unrelenting, invisible battle.

I know this war intimately.

I have lived through it.

And I have refused to let it destroy me.

My journey began in 2006, when an unfamiliar numbness crept into my body. Like a shadow, it never lingered long enough to demand immediate attention, but unsettled me enough so that I started questioning what was happening with my body. By 2009, it took a turn for the worse. The symptoms intensified—numbness, loss of balance, relentless fatigue. My body was betraying me, and no one could tell me why. The darkness was suffocating. I could barely walk. My body felt foreign, broken, disconnected from the very essence of who I was.

The numbness spread; the fear increased. Doctors poked, prodded, tested… And dismissed me. Orthopaedic specialists declared my results "normal". I was left dangling in uncertainty, grasping for answers that seemed just out of reach.

And then, my world changed.

"Probable Autoimmune"

I remember repeatedly asking myself: "What is autoimmune?"

But sometimes, ignorance is bliss. Multiple Sclerosis, Autoimmune... For me, it was all gibberish.

Desperation led me back to yet another doctor, yet another round of tests, yet another kernel of hope that would likely end with the destroyed crop of disappointment. But this time, something was different. This time, one doctor saw beyond the surface. An MRI was ordered, and within moments, my life was split into 'before' and 'after'.

The results were undeniable. Plaques. Scattered across my brain and spine. A silent, merciless attack. Multiple Sclerosis.

With that diagnosis came a whirlwind of hospitalisation, treatments, steroids. With my body swollen, my reflection was unrecognisable. The doctors told me to stop working, to rest, to surrender. "You need to slow down," they said. "Accept your limitations."

But they didn't understand who I was.

I would not slow down. I would not stop. I would not accept a life dictated by a disease.

Instead, I fought harder.

I built a career in the digital world, earning a place among the 'Top 10 Most Powerful Digital Women' and the 'Top 20 International Digital Marketers'. I thrived, not in spite of my illness, but because of my refusal to let it define me. My body was failing, but my spirit? Unbreakable.

But fate wasn't finished with me yet.

As I struggled to manage MS, a new nightmare unfolded. Seventeen times a day, I found myself running to the washroom, my body waging yet another war I didn't understand. Doctors, still fixated on my MS, dismissed it. "It's just a side effect," they said. But I knew better.

I pushed. I demanded answers. I refused to be ignored.

And once again, a brutal truth emerged—Crohn's disease. Another autoimmune disorder. Another relentless adversary.

Paralysis.

Twice.

In two years.

It was just another evening when I tried to get up and felt I numb below my waist. Just about when I was gaining some strength, it struck again. This time, one leg was affected, which was accompanied by low oxygen saturation, almost shifted to the ICU, shortness of breath and Asthma, *and* Psychosomatic Asthma—again something that cannot be treated. I didn't know how long one breath would last or which would be my last breath.

They told me to rest. They told me to accept it. They told me I couldn't keep going.

I proved them wrong.

Through the excruciating pain, the endless hospital stays, the weight gain, the isolation, the misdiagnoses, and the sheer exhaustion of constantly advocating for myself—I kept moving. I kept building. I kept fighting.

I write this book not as a victim, not even as a survivor, but as a warrior. Because autoimmune disease is not just a diagnosis. It's a war. And I refuse to lose.

This is my story. This is my battle cry.

And if you are in this war too, if you are fighting an invisible illness, drowning in pain that no one else can see, wondering if anyone truly understands, know this:

You are not alone.

You are stronger than you think.

And together, we rise.

• • •

THE BEGINNING OF A JOURNEY: A WEIRD START

I grew up in the world of my grandparents. They were my anchors, my home, my entire universe. Like any other child, I believed they would never leave me. That life would always stay the same. That love, in its purest form, was eternal.

They were my formative years.

At 11, I knew and yet I did not. I understood, and yet I did not.

Then, one day, a decision was made.

I was to leave. I was to live with my parents.

The ones who had left me with my grandparents—the ones who visited in the summer, whom I called *Mamma* and *Baba*. The ones who were, by definition, my family but in reality, were just familiar faces.

When the Familiar Feels Foreign

No one asked me what I wanted.

No one thought to sit me down and ask, "Do you want to leave?"

It wasn't a joyous reunion. It wasn't the homecoming that stories speak of. It was betrayal.

I felt abandoned—not by my parents, but by my grandparents. I was angry at them. The ones who had been my world, the ones I had trusted to never let me go.

I was expected to be happy. I was expected to embrace this new life with open arms. But all I felt was loss.

I was moving in with strangers.

They were my family, but I did not know them. I knew their names, their voices, the way they smelled when they held me during those short summer visits. But did I know them? Did they know me?

The walls of their home were different. The rules were different. And yet, the biggest difference was the silence in my heart.

Settling In… Or Pretending To

Slowly, I adjusted.

Because children always do.

My parents ensured that my grandparents were close by. They knew the transition would be hard. My visits back were frequent at first. The gap between the world I had known and the one I was forced to accept was temporarily shortened, and the blow softened.

Then, just as I started finding some footing in this new life, my father made another choice.

He left us.

When Childhood Ends Before it Begins

Life never gave me the luxury of innocence. I was born into love, but I was also born into loss. My story does not begin in a perfect home filled with warmth and stability—it begins with the void left behind when my father, a man of discipline and honour in the Air Force, was taken from us too soon.

He was only 37.

And I was too young to understand what death meant, yet old enough to feel the weight of absence. One moment, I was a little girl safe in the shadow of my father's love. The next, I was thrust into a world that no longer felt safe at all.

But grief doesn't wait for you to be ready. And neither does life.

The world expects children to adapt. To accept. To move forward as though the past does not tug at their small hearts. But here's what no one tells you: Children absorb everything.

We carry the weight of decisions we never made. We internalise the unspoken words, the quiet tensions, the losses that are brushed aside as *necessary change*. I learned that my feelings did not matter. That my voice did not need to be heard. That my pain was an afterthought.

And so, I did what I had learned to do best.

I survived.

Therapist's Reflections: The Emotional Cost of Early Separation

As a psychotherapist, I now understand what my younger self could not:

1. ***Early separations shape attachment styles.*** *When a child is uprooted from a primary caregiver, even with good intentions, it disrupts their sense of security and belonging. This can later manifest as difficulty trusting others, fear of abandonment, or struggles with forming close relationships.*

2. ***Children internalise unspoken pain.*** *Even if no one acknowledges their feelings, children absorb every shift in their environment. The grief of leaving a familiar home, the loneliness of not feeling truly 'seen' by new caregivers—it all leaves an imprint.*

3. ***Survival mode can look like adaptation.*** *A child may appear to settle in, but deep inside, they are often just coping, finding ways to exist in an unfamiliar emotional landscape. Adjusting does not always mean healing.*

Journaling Prompts for Readers

If you have ever experienced a major transition in childhood, take a moment to reflect on these questions. Write freely, without judgment.

1. *Have you ever been in a situation where you had no control over a major life change? How did it shape your sense of security?*

2. *What emotions surface when you think about your childhood home? What does "home" mean to you now?*

3. *If you could go back in time and speak to your younger self during that transition, what would you say to comfort them?*

4. *What does "family" mean to you? Is it based on blood, love, or familiarity?*

5. *Have you ever felt like a guest in a place that was supposed to be home? How did that impact you?*

What are the ways you can create a sense of home and belonging for yourself today?

Before the Next Chapter

Change is inevitable, but how we experience it shapes the way we move through the world.

For me, the transition was not just about leaving my grandparents—it was about leaving behind a version of myself that felt safe, loved, and rooted.

The adjustment was slow, and in many ways, it never truly ended.

But this was only the beginning of understanding what it means to belong as the journey of finding home is not just about a place— it is about finding where your heart feels safe.

Take a moment to breathe, feel, and write. This space is yours.

• • •

A Life Without a Place to Call Home

Losing my father meant losing more than just a parent. It meant losing the only real stability we had. We were uprooted again and again, shuttled between relatives, moving from one place to another, never truly belonging anywhere.

Each new home came with new rules, new expectations and the painful realisation that we were no longer a family in the traditional sense—we were dependents, burdens unloaded from one pair of reluctant hands to another.

Relatives, the ones who should have been our safety net, became our greatest test. Some tolerated us. Some pitied us. And some made sure we knew we were unwanted.

There were houses where I was an afterthought, where I was expected to be grateful just to be under a roof.

There were places where I was the caretaker, the helper, the silent naughty girl who was given no room to just be a child.

And then there were the moments no child should ever have to endure—the moments when trust was shattered by the very people who were supposed to protect me. I learned all too soon that the people you call your own are not always the ones who will keep you safe.

When Innocence is Replaced with Armour

The instability of moving, the cruelty of those who were supposed to care, the silent wounds that could not be spoken aloud—they all shaped me.

I toughened up, not because I wanted to, but because I had to. I was no longer just a girl. I became a fighter.

In a world that constantly tried to push me down, I learned to rear my head. In a space where I was often ignored, I learned to mark my presence. In an environment that wanted me small, I made myself stand out.

I was expected to be grateful for whatever kindness I received, even when it came with conditions. I learned to say "thank you" even when it hurt.

But I learned something else as well.

I learned that pain is a teacher. That hardships are lessons. That every scar I carried would one day be proof that I survived.

I also drew an inference at that young age that life does not wait for children to be ready. That love can exist, yet feel foreign. That family is more than just blood—it is who stands by you, who hears you, who chooses you.

The journey ahead would not be easy. But neither was the one I had already walked.

And through it all, I also learned that belonging is not something given—it is something we fight for.

I did not know it then, but the person I was becoming—the resilient, relentless, unshakable version of myself—was being forged in the fire of those early years.

I did not just survive. I became my own shield.

Therapist's Reflection: The Trauma of a Stolen

Childhood

As a therapist, I now look back on my childhood not just as a survivor, but as an expert in the psychology of trauma.

When children lose a parent early in life, they often experience "emotional parentification"—being forced to grow up too soon.

Moving frequently disrupts a child's sense of safety and belonging, *leading to attachment wounds that last a lifetime.*

Abuse and neglect during childhood can lead to complex PTSD, *affecting self-worth, trust, and relationships well into adulthood.*

But here's what I have learned: Trauma does not have to define us, ***it can refine us.***

Survival does not just mean enduring pain. *It means transforming it.*

Every child who has suffered loss, instability, or betrayal is given two choices:

To let the pain consume them.

To let the pain fuel them.

I chose the second.

And I am here to tell you—you can too.

Journaling Prompts for Readers

If you have experienced childhood trauma, loss, or instability, take a moment to reflect on these questions.

Write freely, without judgment.

1. *What is that one moment from your childhood that shaped the way you see the world today?*

2. *How has pain influenced the way you trust, love, or protect yourself?*

3. *What is the one lesson you have learned from your struggles?*

4. *What is the one thing you would tell your younger self?*

5. *What does resilience mean to you?*

6. *What is the biggest emotional weight you are carrying right now?*

What would happen if you allowed yourself to let go of something that is no longer serving you?

Before the Next Chapter

Looking back, I know that the person I am today was built in those early years. The resilience, the fire, the ability to stand tall facing storms—none of it came from ease.

It came from pain. From struggle. From learning to fight when the world expected me to fall.

This is where my story truly begins.

Not in comfort, but in adversity.

Not in the safety of childhood dreams, but in the reality of battles fought too soon.

But I would not have it any other way.

Because I was born to fight. And I was built to rise.

Take a moment to breathe, feel, and write. This space is yours.

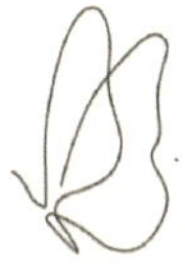

Breaking Points: When Life Pushes You to the Edge

There are moments when life just weighs you down too much, when even the strongest fighters question their own resilience. I have had many such moments, but some left scars so deep that they became turning points in my story.

By the time I reached my teenage years, I had already learned that life was not fair. I had accepted that safety was an illusion, that kindness often came with conditions, and that silence was sometimes the only weapon of survival. But the battles ahead would demand more from me than I ever thought I could give.

Some breaking points come in the form of a single, shattering moment. Others creep up slowly, unnoticed, until one day you wake up and realise you have nothing left to give.

For me, it was both.

Being uprooted again and again does something to you. It teaches you not to get attached, not to expect stability, not to believe that anything is permanent. Every time I started to settle somewhere, every time I allowed myself to believe that maybe, just maybe, this time would be different, life would rip it away.

I learned to pack light—not just my belongings but my emotions, my attachments, my dreams. I built invisible walls around myself, shielding my heart from the inevitable disappointment of losing yet another "home".

And then there was the exhaustion— the emotional and physical exhaustion of constantly adjusting, constantly proving my worth, constantly trying to fit into places that were never truly mine. I was expected to be grateful for whatever I got, no matter how little, no matter how much it cost me. I was taught to say "thank you" even when kindness was laced with cruelty.

I carried those moments in my bones, in my breath, in the spaces between my words. I buried them deep, because that's what survivors do. We do not break. We adapt. We learn to live with the weight of things no one should have to carry.

Looking back, I realise that survival had become my identity. I had learned to exist without expecting safety. To keep my emotions light because attachments were too heavy. To accept love, even when it was given half-heartedly, as asking for more was a risk I felt I could not afford.

I had convinced myself that I was strong because I endured. But strength is not about how much you can carry. It is about knowing when to put it down.

And one day, I would have to decide—would I continue walking through life carrying the weight of every loss, every disappointment, every betrayal?

Or would I finally allow myself the freedom to let it go?

Therapist's Reflection: The Emotional Cost of Survival

As a psychotherapist, I now understand what my younger self never could:

1. ***Constant instability rewires the brain to expect loss.*** *When a child is uprooted over and over, they learn not to trust permanence. This can lead to emotional detachment, struggles with commitment, and difficulty forming deep connections later in life.*

2. ***Being grateful and being treated fairly are not the same thing.*** *Many who experience instability or emotional neglect are conditioned to accept whatever they receive—even if it comes with conditions, manipulation, or pain.*

3. ***The weight of survival is exhausting.*** *When every day feels like a fight to prove your worth, burnout is inevitable. Emotional and physical exhaustion are not signs of weakness; they are signs that you have been carrying too much for too long.*

Journaling Prompts for Readers

If you have ever felt like you had to carry too much, take a moment to reflect on these questions. Write freely, without judgment.

1. *Have you ever felt like you had to accept less than you deserved just to keep the peace? How did that impact you?*

2. *What emotions have you suppressed in order to appear strong?*

3. *What would it feel like to put down the weight you've been carrying?*

4. *If you could go back and comfort your younger self, what would you say to them?*

5. *Have you ever mistaken endurance for strength? How has that shaped your choices?*

6. *Do you struggle with believing that stability is possible for you? Why or why not?*

7. *What does it mean to you to feel truly at home—emotionally, mentally and physically?*

8. *What is the one step you can take today to allow yourself to feel safe, seen, and valued?*

Before the Next Chapter

Children feel deeply, even when they don't have words to express it.

Being part of a family does not always mean feeling at home.

A child's emotions should never be dismissed as "they'll get over it".

We may not have control over the past, but we have control over how we heal.

Healing is possible.

Understanding our past is the first step in reclaiming our voice.

Take a moment to breathe, feel, and write. This space is yours.

TEENAGE YEARS: THE SILENT WARS

If childhood was a battlefield, my teenage years were a silent war.

By this stage, I was no longer the little girl lost between homes, nor was I the child waiting for life to get easier. I had long accepted that life was not fair, that stability was a privilege I was never meant to have. But adolescence brought a new kind of struggle—one that was less about external circumstances and more about the internal wars that raged inside me.

Growing Up Before My Time

While most teenagers navigated friendships, school, and the innocence of first loves, I

was navigating something else entirely. I was learning how to build walls so high that no one could reach me. I was learning that pain does not always come from fists—it comes from words, from silence, from being invisible even when you're screaming inside.

I had perfected the art of survival. I had learned to smile when I was breaking. To speak in a way that made others comfortable while suppressing my own discomfort. To become what was expected of me: A responsible, independent girl who needed no one.

But inside, I was carrying too much.

Years of instability, of being moved from place to place, of never truly knowing what *home* meant, had left their imprint on me. I didn't trust easily. I didn't allow myself to get too attached. Not because I didn't crave connection—but because I had learned that attachment was always accompanied by a cost.

I built walls. Not because I wanted to, but because I had to.

The Escape into Books and Achievement

School was my only sanctuary. Books didn't judge me. Knowledge didn't reject me. Between the pages of my textbooks, I could be *anyone*.

I wasn't just the girl with invisible scars.

I wasn't just the girl who had seen too much, too soon. I worked harder than most.

Excellence wasn't an option—it was survival. I knew that if I wanted a way out, education was my only ticket.

However, in school, I played another role.

I was the carefree girl gossiping about crushes. I was sneaking out for adventures, dreaming about fairy-tale romances. And yet—I was focused, relentless, unstoppable.

I lived two lives. One that the world saw. And one that I carried inside.

A Love that Found Me Too Soon

And yet, despite it all—I still longed for normalcy. I still wanted to belong.

I was loved by many. Especially the ones who weren't tied to me by blood, by obligation, by expectations.

This was when I met my husband. We were just 15!

Even then, I didn't believe in love—not the kind they spoke about in stories.

But I believed in friendship. In loyalty. In someone who saw me for who I was, not just what I had been through.

I didn't have time to be young.

I was too busy trying to survive.

Loneliness in a Crowd

Despite the noise, despite the people, loneliness never left me. I was surrounded by crowds, yet I stood behind a glass wall.

Watching.

Observing.

Seeing people live a life I could never quite touch. Teenage years are supposed to be about self-discovery. For me? Self-discovery wasn't a privilege—it was a necessity. I had to figure out how to navigate a world where I had no safety net, where mistakes were not an option, where every decision I made could determine whether I sank or swam.

And so, I chose to swim.

And then, I swam.

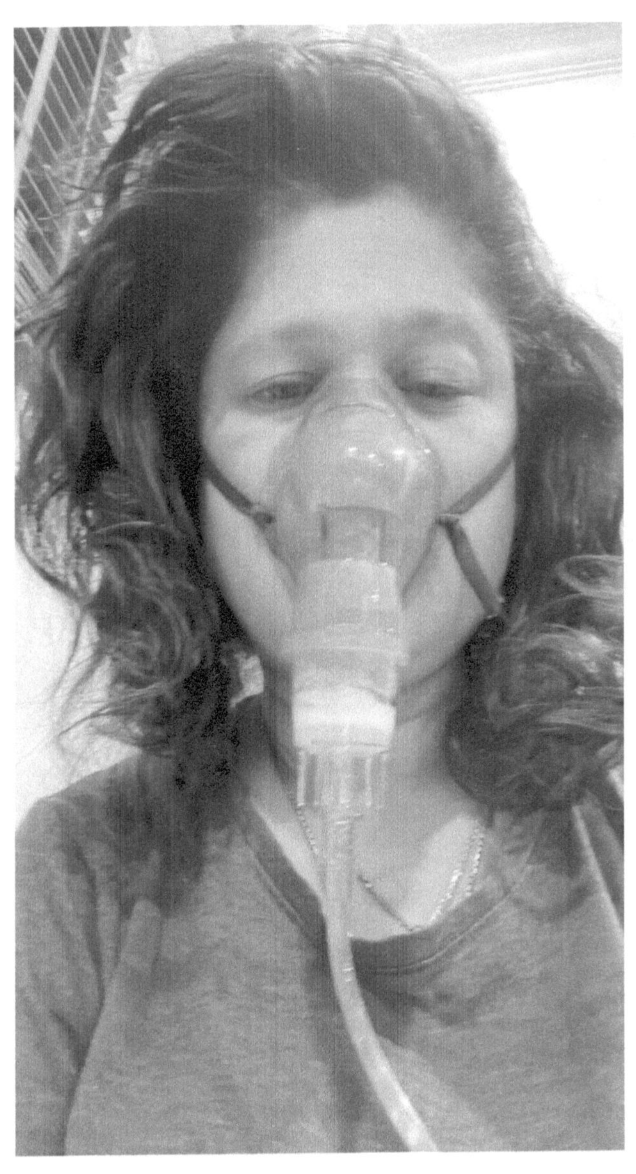

Looking Back: The Weight of Wearing a Mask

Looking back, I now see: I wasn't just surviving. I was performing.

Performing strength. Performing independence. Performing the version of myself that the world expected.

I had convinced myself that if I just kept going, kept excelling, kept pretending—no one would see the cracks beneath the surface.

But the truth is—strength does not come from silence.

Strength comes from knowing when to take the mask off.

And one day, life would teach me the hardest lesson of all: No matter how well you master the art of survival, the body, the mind and the soul will eventually demand to be seen.

The question is—when the weight of the mask becomes too heavy, will you have the courage to take it off?

Therapist's Reflection: When Survival Becomes Isolation

As a psychotherapist, I now understand what my younger self never could:

1. **Perfectionism is often a shield for trauma.** *Many overachievers aren't just ambitious—they are running from something. Their success is built upon the fear of being powerless again.*

2. **Loneliness doesn't mean being alone— it means feeling unseen.** *You can be surrounded by love and still feel isolated if no one truly understands your battles.*

3. **Survival mode teaches you to keep moving, but healing requires you to stop.** *You cannot outrun trauma. No*

amount of achievements, distractions, or relationships will make it disappear. It waits—until you are ready to face it.

Journaling Prompts for Readers

If you have ever felt like you had to wear a mask to protect yourself, take a moment to reflect on these questions. Write freely, without judgment.

1. *Have you ever felt like you had to be strong for others while hiding your own struggles? What did that feel like?*

2. *Do you find yourself keeping people at a distance, even when you crave a connection? Why do you think that is?*

3. *If you could tell your teenage self one thing, what would it be?*

4. *Have you ever mistaken independence for strength? How has that shaped your relationships?*

5. *If you could unlearn one belief about yourself that was shaped by your past, what would it be?*

Before the Next Chapter

Wearing a mask may protect you, but it also isolates you.

Loneliness is not about the number of people around you—it's about whether you feel understood.

Survival mode can push you forward, but it can also keep you from truly living.

Sometimes, love finds you before you're ready. And sometimes, it teaches you what readiness really means.

Take a moment to breathe, feel, and write. This space is yours.

LOVE, LOSS AND THE BATTLE WITHIN

Love stepped into my life, in the most unexpected manner. A love that taught me, broke me and rebuilt me in ways I never imagined.

Love has a strange way of finding you when you least expect it. It doesn't announce itself with grand gestures or dramatic moments like in the movies. Sometimes, it comes in quietly, disguised as friendship, comfort, or the feeling of finally being understood.

That's how it was with him.

I met him during my teenage years, at a time when my world had already taught me not to trust too easily, not to rely on the permanence of people. At first, it was just a crush—a fleeting admiration, something I told myself would pass like all the other small distractions of youth.

But with him, something felt different.

With him, I didn't have to be strong all the time. I didn't have to explain myself, didn't have to carry the weight of my past or pretend to be someone I wasn't. There was a quiet safety in his presence, an ease that I had never felt before.

For the first time in my life, I had found a place where I didn't need to fight.

A Natural Transition

Our relationship began in the most unassuming manner. There was no rush, no urgency—just two people who found solace in each other's company. He became the one I could talk to without filters, the one who saw me not as the girl who had survived too much but simply as me.

And without realising it, without intending for it to happen, that friendship turned into something deeper.

And so, we built something that neither of us had planned.

Love wasn't something I had ever put much thought into. I had been too busy surviving, too consumed with trying to hold my world together. But life, as it always does, had its own plans.

And one day, without any dramatic declarations or carefully rehearsed moments, I realised—I didn't just like him. I loved him.

We married young, against the usual advice to wait, to experience more of life first. But we didn't need to wait. We had already seen enough, fought enough battles separately to know that whatever life had in store, we wanted to face it together.

From that love, our two greatest blessings were born—our son and our daughter.

Raising them was not just a responsibility; it was the greatest purpose of my life. As I watched them grow, I took pride not just in who they were becoming, but in the way we had raised them. Despite everything, we built a family filled with love, understanding, and resilience. Though most often I was nothing but an onlooker as my ailments demanded more time.

Though yes, I did manage to teach my children to be moral, ethical and always be true to their values. They know that lies—active or by omission—will not allow them to face their own reflection in the mirror.

New Life, New Rules, New Lessons

Marriage was supposed to be a sanctuary, a place where love and commitment created a foundation stronger than anything the world could throw at us. But soon after our wedding, I learned a truth that too many women discover after saying "I do".

Marriage was not just about love. It was about constant adjustments.

It was about realising that the family I thought I knew—the one I had been embraced by for years—was not what I had imagined.

It was about discovering that no matter how much love exists between two people, the weight of expectations, traditions and unwritten rules could suffocate even the strongest.

Friends and Frenemies

I have been blessed with some beautiful friends since decades. Some are still rock-solid. Sadly, many turned out to be opportunists. The gradual toxicity that marred those friendships compelled me to amputate that part of my life.

I finally realised that even friendship comes at a cost. The most malignant of them make you question your life choices. Betrayal, games, narcissism, manipulation… I dealt with the entire gamut of negative emotions when a so-called best friend couldn't stand up for our friendship. It hurt me then. It hurts me now. I forgave, not for anything else but just because I didn't want to carry that baggage anymore.

While navigating the maze of marriage, I was also busy carrying the burden of this situational relationship with a man I once thought was my best friend. I then realised that my self-respect trumps conditions, disclaimers and insults a typical narcissist dishes out. Perhaps he did not have a voice of his own, perhaps his words meant nothing, perhaps he had some agenda.

But that's life and he holds no place in mine now. Instead, now that I think I have hit rock bottom, I cherish the ones who are there, the ones who always have been there, the ones who always will be there…

So you see, I didn't have time to be young. I was too busy trying to survive.

Therapist's Reflection: Not all Who Appear Close are Meant to Stay

As a psychotherapist, I now understand what my younger self never could:

1. **People who learn to wear a mask of strength often do so out of necessity, not choice.** *When survival requires constant adaptation, vulnerability feels like a risk too great to take.*

2. **Loneliness does not always mean being alone.** *You can be surrounded by people, deeply loved and still feel isolated if you don't allow yourself to be fully seen.*

3. **Betrayal from those we trust is one of the deepest wounds.** *When relationships built on love and trust unravel, they leave scars that take years to heal—if we let ourselves acknowledge them at all.*

4. ***Letting go of toxic relationships is an act of self-respect.*** *It takes strength to recognise when certain people no longer belong in our lives, and even more strength to walk away from them.*

5. ***Friendships, like love, should be nurturing—not a transaction.*** *If a relationship consistently drains more than it gives, it may not be worth holding on to.*

6. ***Being "strong" does not mean ignoring your pain.*** *True strength is being able to acknowledge when something is breaking you.*

7. ***The people who stay when you are at your lowest are the ones who were always meant to be there.***

Journaling Prompts for Readers

If you have ever struggled with masking your pain, reflect on these questions. Write freely, without judgment.

1. *Have you ever maintained a friendship or relationship out of obligation rather than genuine connection? How did it affect you?*

2. *What is one relationship in your life that has stood the test of time? What makes it different from the ones that fell apart?*

3. *Have you ever felt the need to wear a "mask of strength" to protect yourself? What would it take for you to remove it?*

4. *If you could go back and give advice to your teenage self, what would you say about love, friendships, and trust?*

Before the Next Chapter

Looking back, I realise I let people into my life, but only on my terms, only within the walls I built around myself. I told myself that as long as I could laugh with them, as long as I could hold on to moments of joy, I was safe.

But trust is not built on temporary moments—it is built on consistency, on truth, on a shared understanding that no one has to pretend.

And when I finally stopped pretending, when I let go of the ones who were never truly there for me, something unexpected happened.

I made space for the ones who were.

Because strength is not about holding on to everything—it is about knowing when to let go.

Take a moment to breathe, feel, and write. This space is yours.

____

____

____

____

____

____

____

____

____

First Blow: Burned, But Not Broken

L ife has a way of tearing away our illusions, of stripping us down to our most raw, most vulnerable selves. And sometimes, it does so in fire.

Scars in the Firelight

Some scars come quietly, like cracks forming in the soul. Others arrive screaming—in fire, in betrayal, in agony.

Mine came twice. Both times, uninvited. Both times, unforgettable.

The first time it happened, it was just a regular day. I was using a steamer. Boiling water. Nothing seemed unusual. Until my skin felt like it was melting. The pain was instant, searing. But it was brushed off. "Just a first-degree burn," they said.

But it wasn't.

In the hours that followed, the burn worsened. Infection set in. Fever. Swelling. Screaming pain. I was admitted to the hospital. Not to heal—but to suffer.

The doctor didn't see a woman in pain. He saw an opportunity. I wasn't treated—I was used. No anaesthesia. No explanation. Just a schedule of suffering. Every alternate day, he would take me to the OT, scrape my wound without warning, without empathy, then wrap me in layers of gauze as if my pain was irrelevant.

I was cleaned before surgery without sedation. My screams echoed in the hospital halls. I begged. I thrashed. I cried for help. But no one came.

Pain that acute doesn't fade. It embeds itself in your muscles, your memory, your bones. And what hurt most wasn't the fire on my skin—it was the silence around it. The absence of compassion. The brutality of being unseen in your agony.

The Fire Rages On

Just when I thought I had endured enough, the second incident knocked like fate's cruel encore.

My son was seven months old. I was still nursing him. Still trying to be a mother through my body's daily betrayals. One morning, while the domestic help was cleaning, a vessel brimming with boiling tea accidentally slipped from her fingers and splashed down. On me.

The tea—blazing, violent—spilled down my lower back.

I screamed again. This time, not just from the pain but from heartbreak. I couldn't hold my baby. Couldn't comfort him. Couldn't even let him touch me without jolting from the rawness of my own skin.

But this time, I wasn't alone.

Two doctor friends—blessings in human form—came to my rescue. They treated me at home with compassion, dignity and care that felt like a balm not just to the wounds on my back but to the wounds in my spirit.

And yet—the fire had done its work.

It didn't just burn my skin. It burned away every illusion I'd held about control, safety, predictability. I thought I'd already faced my greatest battles—Multiple Sclerosis, Crohn's Disease, hospitalisations, depression, ECTs. But fire? It demanded something different. A surrender. A rebirth.

The burn ward was something out of a nightmare. The smell—charred flesh, sterile antiseptic, and something darker… Despair. The air was thick with the scent of scorched flesh, sterile antiseptics, and something far worse—the lingering echoes of suffering. The cries of patients, their raw agony piercing through the cold hospital walls, were inescapable.

Those weren't just sounds—they were reminders. Of how close we live to destruction. Of how fast a body can betray. Of how trauma is both intimate and collective.

I remember once being wheeled past a young girl, her face completely charred, crying for her mother. That moment broke something in me. I wasn't the only one in pain. I wasn't the worst case. And yet, the cruelty I experienced—the negligence, the silence—felt inhumane.

You learn, after surviving burns, that healing doesn't mean restoration. It means reinvention. My scars did not fade. They stayed. They whispered.

But they also made me powerful.

Moments of Agony

Two separate accidents. Two moments of agony that would etch themselves into my flesh and my memory. The flames didn't just sear my skin—they burned away the false sense of control I had clung to for so long. In an instant, I was reminded of a truth I had spent my life refusing to accept: Nothing is permanent. Not comfort. Not safety. Not even the body I had always believed would carry me forward, strong and unyielding.

I thought I had faced my greatest test when I was diagnosed with Multiple Sclerosis and Crohn's Disease. I thought my body had endured enough betrayal. But I was wrong.

Every time they wheeled me out of my ward, I saw them—the others. Faces disfigured, skin melted into grotesque shapes, eyes that held more suffering than any words could express. Some of them would never walk out. Some of them would never see their own reflection the same way again.

I was one of the lucky ones.

And then, as if fate had decided I had suffered enough, help came. The two doctors, strangers at the time, risked everything to intervene. They saw through the lies, the deception, the greed. They knew I didn't belong there any longer, and they acted—not just as doctors, but as warriors of justice in a system that so often fails those who need it most.

They fought for me. They stood up against their own, risking their careers to ensure that I walked out of that hospital. They didn't just save me—they gave me back my faith in humanity.

That was over 30 years ago. Today, those doctors are no longer just memories of a dark time. They are family. We live in different cities now, separated by miles but bound by something stronger than blood. Loyalty. Love. A shared understanding of what it means to stand on the edge of suffering and pull someone back before they fall too far.

But as much as that experience shaped me, as much as it left its scars—both visible and unseen—it was not the greatest battle of my life.

No, life wasn't done with me yet.

The war was far from over.

And I was just getting started.

Therapist's Reflection: When Fire Burns More Than Skin

As a psychotherapist, I now understand what trauma in its rawest form can do to the body, the mind and the soul:

1. ***Physical trauma doesn't heal in isolation.*** *The body may recover, but the emotional toll often lingers far longer. Burns especially are not just skin-deep—they reshape identity, self-image, and safety.*

2. ***Institutional betrayal compounds trauma.*** *When those entrusted with your care cause harm—through neglect, greed,*

or indifference—it leaves a deeper, more invisible scar. That betrayal teaches you not just to fear pain, but to question trust.

3. **Rescue creates lifelong bonds.** In moments of utter vulnerability, the people who show up, who risk something for you, who act with integrity—those people redefine the meaning of love, safety, and faith in humanity.

Journaling Prompts for Readers

If you've ever been through physical or emotional trauma, or had to rely on others to protect you when you couldn't protect yourself, reflect on these. Write without judgment.

Have you ever felt completely powerless in a situation that was supposed to be safe? What helped you through it?

Was there someone who stepped in when you needed help the most? How did that act of support shape your view of people?

What moments in your life felt like they stripped away your control? How did you regain your sense of self?

Are there people in your life today you consider "chosen family"? How were those bonds formed?

Before the next Chapter

Some pain doesn't just hurt—it humbles. *It breaks you down, strips away illusions, and shows you who you are when there's nothing left to hold onto.*

Hospitals are supposed to heal, but sometimes, they're where the greatest harm happens. *Healing isn't always about treatment— it's about who is treating you and why.*

True loyalty is born in chaos. *The people who rescue you in your darkest moments don't just enter your life—they etch themselves into your soul.*

The human spirit can be seared, but it can't be erased. *Even in agony, even in betrayal, there is space for faith, for hope, for fight.*

Somatic & Healing Exercises

1. **Fire Release Ritual (Candle Practice)**
Light a candle in a quiet space. With each breath, release memories of pain. Say aloud:

   - "This flame is not to burn me, but to remind me—I am light too."

   - Journal what emotions come up as you watch the flame.

   - Optional: Write your pain on a piece of paper and safely burn it in a fire-safe bowl.

2. **Trauma Trace Body Sketch**

   - Draw or outline your body. On one side, mark where pain or trauma lives. On the other, where you feel strength or resilience. Name each spot. What do these parts want to say to you?

3. **Mirror Healing Affirmations**

- Stand before a mirror. Gently touch your scars (physical or emotional). Say:

- "You did nothing to deserve this."

- "You were not weak. You were wounded."

- "You are allowed to heal at your pace."

4. **Caregiver Reframe Exercise**

- List the people who showed up. What did they do right? What made it healing?

- Write a thank-you note to them (even if you never send it). Let it be a release.

5. **Reparenting Inner Voice Work**

- Close your eyes. Imagine your burned, broken self. Now imagine an older, wiser version of you holding her. What would you say? Say it out loud. Write it down. That's your new inner voice.

Take a moment to breathe, feel, and write. This space is yours.

____

____

____

____

____

____

____

____

____

____

Looking Back: The Fire that Forged Me

I thought surviving the burns was the hardest part. I thought the physical pain was the real test.

But I had no idea. I now understand that the fire that burned me also revealed me.

It stripped away everything I thought I knew about myself, about life, about control.

It forced me to see the truth—that no matter how strong we are, we all need saving sometimes.

But more than anything, it taught me this:

Scars are not just reminders of pain.

They are proof that we walked through the fire and survived.

The Unspoken Trauma

But just because I chose to survive didn't mean I was unscathed. There were parts of my past that I had buried so deeply I refused to acknowledge them. The moments of mistreatment, the times I was made to feel small, the violations of trust that I had endured in silence.

I didn't talk about them.

I didn't allow myself to think about them.

Instead, I turned my pain into ambition. I worked harder. I built a persona so strong that no one would ever see the cracks beneath it. If I could just keep moving forward, maybe—just maybe—I could outrun my past.

But trauma is not something you can escape. It stays in your body, in your mind, in the way you react to the world around you.

It manifests in the way you hesitate before trusting.

It shows up in the way you flinch at unexpected kindness.

It controls the way you hold yourself together even when everything inside you is falling apart.

At the time, I didn't have the words for it.

I only knew that I had to keep going.

The question is, when the mask finally cracks, will you be ready to face what's underneath? The the scars left on the body heal with time. The scars left on the soul—they take far longer.

Therapist's Reflection: When Trauma Becomes a Teacher

As a psychotherapist, I now understand what my younger self never could:

1. ***Pain does not come alone—it changes everything.*** *Traumatic events don't just leave physical scars; they alter the way we see the world, trust others, and perceive our own resilience.*

2. ***Not all wounds are visible.*** *Some of the deepest scars are the ones no one can see—the ones we carry in silence, in our memories, in the way we react to life long after the event has passed.*

3. ***There is no shame in being saved.*** *Sometimes, we need others to step in when we cannot save ourselves. Strength is not just about enduring—it is also about accepting help when it is given.*

Journaling Prompts for Readers

If you have ever survived something that left lasting scars, take a moment to reflect on these questions. Write freely, without judgment.

1. *What is one painful event in your life that changed you? How did you come out of it?*

2. *Have you ever felt trapped in a situation where someone else had to step in to help you? How did that make you feel?*

3. *Do you carry emotional scars that others cannot see? How do they still affect you today?*

4. *If you could rewrite your relationship with pain, what would that look like?*

Before the Next Chapter

Survival is not just about making it through the worst—it is about finding meaning in what remains.

Not all angels have wings—sometimes, they wear doctor's coats.

Pain has the power to break you or to shape you. The choice is yours.

Some scars are not reminders of pain, but of battles we have won.

Take a moment to breathe, feel, and write. This space is yours.

THE BIRTH OF A FIGHTER

If my childhood had taught me to endure, my teenage years taught me to fight.

- Not with my fists, not with anger, but with relentless resilience.

- I fought through every obstacle, through every setback, through every moment that tried to break me.

- I fought against the narrative that I was just another girl with a tragic story.

- I fought for my future.

And in doing so, I discovered something that would shape the rest of my life: I was not just someone who had survived. I was someone who would rise. Again and again. No matter how many times life tried to push me down.

I didn't know it then, but this unshakable will to keep going, this refusal to let circumstances define me, would one day become my greatest strength.

It was the beginning of something bigger.

But first, there was still more to endure, but with

relentless resilience.

I fought through every obstacle.

Through every betrayal.

Through every attempt to break me.

I didn't know it then, but this refusal to surrender, this fire that refused to die, would become my greatest weapon.

It was the beginning of something far greater than survival.

Looking Back: The Art of Rising

Looking back, I realise now that I was never fighting for success. I was fighting to prove that I was more than the pain that tried to define me.

I was never fighting for validation. I was fighting to reclaim what was taken from me— my voice, my dignity, my power.

I was never fighting for survival.

I was fighting for the right to rise.

And the world was about to learn that I don't stay down for long.

I realise now that every battle I faced was leading me somewhere. At the time, all I knew was that I had to keep going—that stopping was not an option. I had no roadmap, no guarantees, just an unshakable instinct that told me: You are not done yet.

I didn't just want to survive—I wanted to win.

But here's what no one tells you about being a fighter:

The hardest fight is not with the world. It is with yourself.

Therapist's Reflection: When Survival Becomes a Battlefield

As a psychotherapist, I now understand what my younger self never could:

1. **Ambition can be a trauma response.** *Many high achievers are not just driven by passion—they are driven by a deep fear of being powerless again. Success becomes their shield.*

2. **Betrayal by the systems we trust—whether family, society, or corporations—leaves lasting wounds.** *When those meant to support us instead discard us, we learn to depend on no one.*

3. ***Walking away from injustice is not weakness.*** *Knowing when to leave, when to stop fighting for people who will never see your worth, is one of the hardest lessons to learn.*

Journaling Prompts for Readers

If you have ever felt like you had to prove your worth to those who never deserved you, take a moment to reflect on these questions. Write freely, without judgment.

Have you ever been underestimated or dismissed despite your efforts? How did it affect you?

What does ambition mean to you? Is it something you chase for passion, or is it something that protects you?

What is one thing from your past that still haunts you today? How does it show up in your life?

If you could reclaim one thing—one part of yourself—that you lost in the fight, what would it be?

Have you ever mistaken survival for success?

Before the Next Chapter

You can be strong and still carry wounds no one sees.

Some fights are not worth fighting—some battles are won by walking away.

Your worth is not determined by the people who fail to recognize it.

You are not defined by what you lost, but by what you refused to let go of—yourself.

Take a moment to breathe, feel, and write. This space is yours.

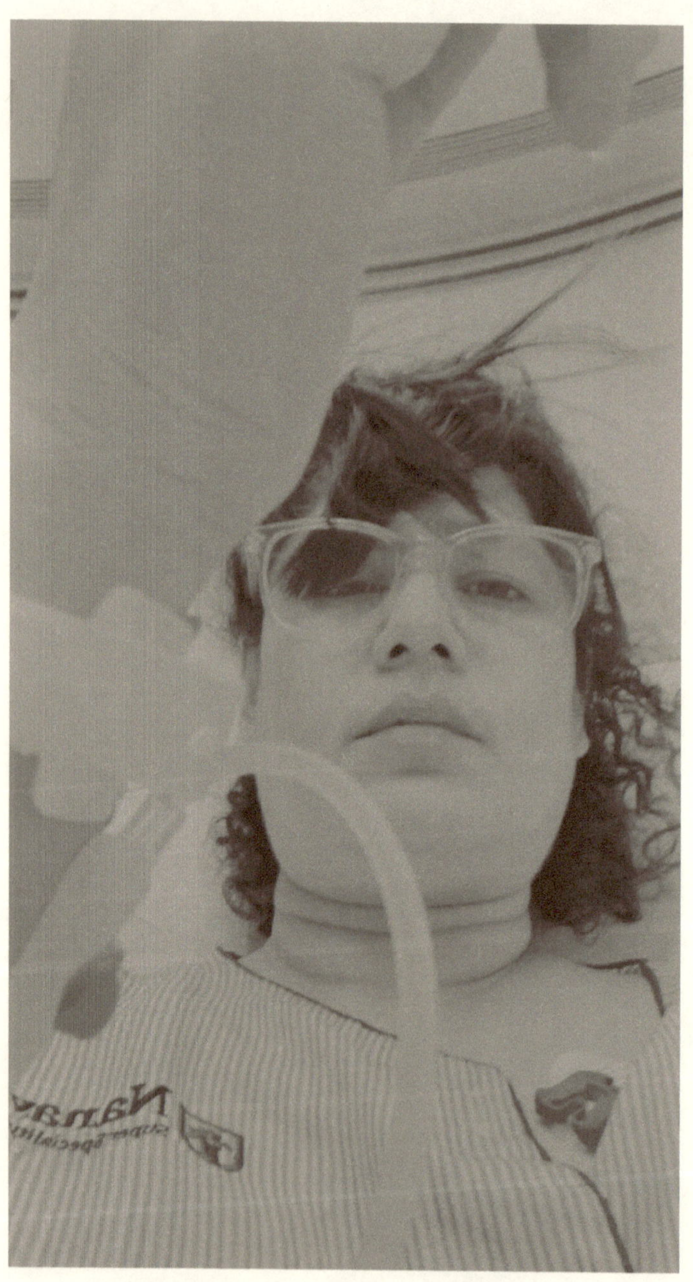

When the Body Fights Back: The Invisible Wounds of Change

Our body has a way of remembering, even when the mind tries to forget. When severe clinical depression, with eight electric shocks—not long after my marriage—Multiple Sclerosis, Crohn's Disease and Psychosomatic Asthma came crashing into my life, I realised something: My body had been fighting battles long before the doctors ever gave them names.

Depression was one of those incidents again where I failed to stand up for myself when I was physically abused, unexpected in today's generation, after marriage with two infants in my marital house which I still can't call a home even after 30 years.

Yes! I do remember there was no one, not one elder in the family (apart from my grandmother) who stood up for me or held the hand of that person, and it looked like a perfect circus with two infants of mine and another two kids a little older watching the drama. Till date, this incident is a joke for many in-house.

I wonder why I feared whom I did fear? Why did I not say how dare you? But today I know when and where to stand up for. It does not matter young or old, torture is torture. Physical, emotional or psychological, which slowly becomes a trauma.

Chronic illness didn't just appear out of nowhere. It was a culmination of years of survival, years of stress, years of holding everything inside with no outlet. It was as if my body had finally decided it had enough, that it could no longer keep up with the weight of what it had endured.

For so long, I had relied on my strength. I had carried myself through life with grit, with resilience, with an unbreakable will to keep going. And now, suddenly, my own body was turning against me.

The fighter in me refused to accept it. I was in denial. I ignored the signs, dismissed the warnings, convinced myself that if I just pushed harder, fought harder, I could outrun the inevitable.

I was wrong.

No matter how strong you are, no matter how much you've endured, life has a way of reminding you that even warriors have limits.

The Moment that Changed Everything

If I had to pick one moment—the moment when I realised I could not keep living the way

I had—it was when my body finally gave up on me.

I remember the exhaustion so deep it felt like drowning. The days when even getting out of bed felt like a war. The slow, creeping realisation that this was not something I could fight my way through with sheer willpower.

For the first time in my life, I felt helpless.

For the first time in my life, I had to ask myself: What if I can't do this? What if this is the battle I finally lose?

And that was when I realised something even more terrifying than illness itself—I had spent my entire life fighting, but I had never truly learned how to heal.

I had survived everything thrown at me, but I had never learned how to rest, how to be at peace, how to allow myself the grace of softness.

This was the breaking point that changed everything.

It was not the moment I lost.

It was the moment I realised that strength is not just about fighting. It is also about knowing when to let go.

It was the moment I understood that my journey was not just about enduring. It was about learning how to rise

The Weight of Silence

I now see that my teenage years were not just about growing up—they were about surviving in silence.

I built walls around myself so no one could see the cracks. I smiled when I was breaking. I carried burdens no child should have to bear.

I thought I was protecting myself.

But what I was really doing was keeping myself from healing.

Pain does not disappear when ignored. It waits. It settles deep in the bones, in the heart, in the spaces where words were never spoken.

And that is about pain, it demands to be felt.

The question is—when the weight of silence becomes too heavy, will you finally allow yourself to let it go?

I now realise that my body had been trying to warn me for years.

It whispered through fatigue. It tightened with stress. It screamed through illness.

But I didn't listen.

Because I thought strength meant pushing through. I thought warriors never stopped.

I was wrong.

The body will always demand to be heard. If we do not listen, it will force us to.

And that day—when exhaustion overtook me, when I could no longer fight back—I finally understood: The battle is not won by fighting endlessly. It is won by knowing when to surrender to healing.

Therapist's Reflection: When the Body Speaks the Mind's Pain

As a psychotherapist, I now understand what my younger self never could:

1. **The body always keeps score.** *Unprocessed trauma, chronic stress, and years of emotional suppression don't just vanish—they manifest as illness, fatigue, and pain. The body carries what the mind tries to forget.*

2. ***Silence is not protection.*** *Enduring abuse—physical, emotional, or psychological—without speaking up does not make you stronger; it only teaches your nervous system that suffering is normal. But suffering should never be normalized.*

3. ***Denial does not prevent the inevitable.*** *Ignoring the warning signs of emotional and physical exhaustion does not mean they disappear. It only means the reckoning will come harder, forcing you to confront what you tried to outrun.*

Journaling Prompts for Readers

If you have ever felt like your body was carrying a weight you couldn't explain, take a moment to reflect on these questions. Write freely, without judgment.

1. *Have you ever ignored signs from your body that something was wrong? What were they?*

2. *What emotional pain do you think your body has carried for you over the years?*

3. *If you could give your past self-permission to rest, to stop fighting just for a moment, what would you say?*

4. *How can you begin to listen to your body's signals and treat yourself with more care?*

5. *Have you ever mistaken physical exhaustion for emotional strength?*

6. *What does healing mean to you? Have you ever allowed yourself to fully embrace it?*

7. *Do you believe you are allowed to rest? Or do you feel like stopping is the same as giving up?*

Before the Next Chapter

Trauma does not just live in the mind—it embeds itself into the body. *Illness, exhaustion and chronic pain are often the echoes of battles fought long ago.*

True healing is not just about surviving—it is about unlearning the belief that suffering is required for strength.

Knowing when to let go is just as important as knowing when to fight. Not every battle is meant to be won by endurance alone.

You are not weak for breaking down. You are human. And even warriors need rest.

Take a moment to breathe, feel, and write. This space is yours.

• • •

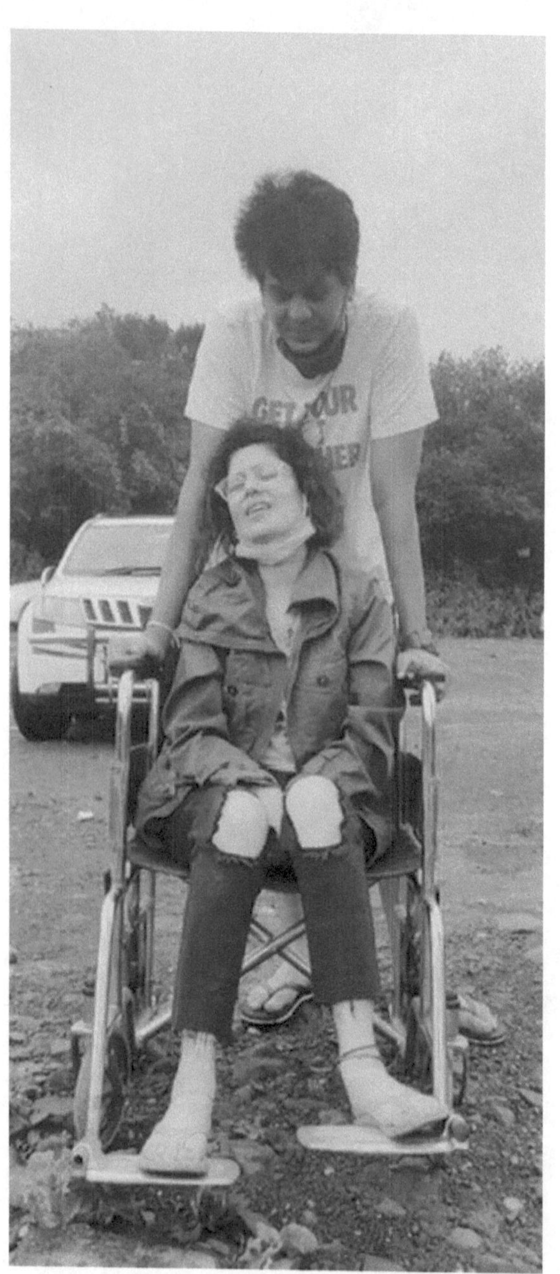

THE WOUNDS THAT DON'T FADE

Just because I survived didn't mean I was untouched. Some scars don't just invade the skin—they live in the silence of things left unsaid, in the weight of moments too painful to hold, in the trust that was shattered before it had a chance to grow.

I buried those parts of my past so deep that even I couldn't reach them. The mistreatment. The times I was made to feel small. The betrayals disguised as love.

I didn't talk about them.

I didn't even let myself think about them.

Instead, I turned my pain into ambition. I worked harder. Built myself from the ground up. Reinvented every broken piece of me into something unbreakable. If I could just keep moving, if I could just stay ahead, maybe—just maybe—I could outrun the ghosts of my past.

But trauma doesn't work that way. It stays on your breath when you hesitate before trusting someone. It lingers in the way you flinch at unexpected kindness. It controls the way you smile when everything inside you is falling apart.

And when the world thought they could take everything from me, I proved them wrong.

I **built** me.

When I stepped into the digital world, I didn't know what my passion was. I didn't know what I was meant for. But the moment I was introduced to the industry, I knew—*THIS IS IT.*

And for two decades, I carved my name into that space. They called me one of India's Top 10 Powerful Digital Women. They ranked me among the Top 20 International Marketers.

And yet, when my symptoms worsened, when my body demanded mercy, the so-called corporate world—the one I had given everything to—had no place for me.

They didn't understand autoimmune disorders. They didn't understand pain that doesn't show on the surface. They didn't understand the warrior who was wheeled into meetings, who still closed deals, who still built empires from battlefields.

Instead, they ridiculed me.

No explanation. No consideration. Just blatant disregard for human dignity. I fought back. I filed a case. I made sure they knew I would not go quietly.

But some battles aren't worth fighting forever. So, I chose to walk away.

But what hurt the most was not leaving the job. It was the helplessness of knowing that I could work, that my brain functioned perfectly, but in a world ruled by opportunists, disability is seen as weakness.

They refused to pay me. Fifteen months' salary—stolen.

But I let them keep it.

I believe in charity.

Because I had already decided—I would not fight for crumbs. I would not beg for respect from people who could never see my worth.

I walked away.

Because my war was not with them. It was with something far greater.

The Descent into Darkness

There is a kind of exhaustion that no amount of sleep can fix. A kind of heaviness that sits in your bones, in your breath, in the spaces between your words.

Depression is not just sadness. It is nothingness.

It is feeling that the world is moving around you while you remain still, untouched, as if you are watching your own life from a distance.

At first, I ignored it.

I had survived worse, hadn't I? What was this compared to everything else I had endured?

But depression doesn't care how strong you are.

The weight of expectations, of disappointments, of a life that no longer felt

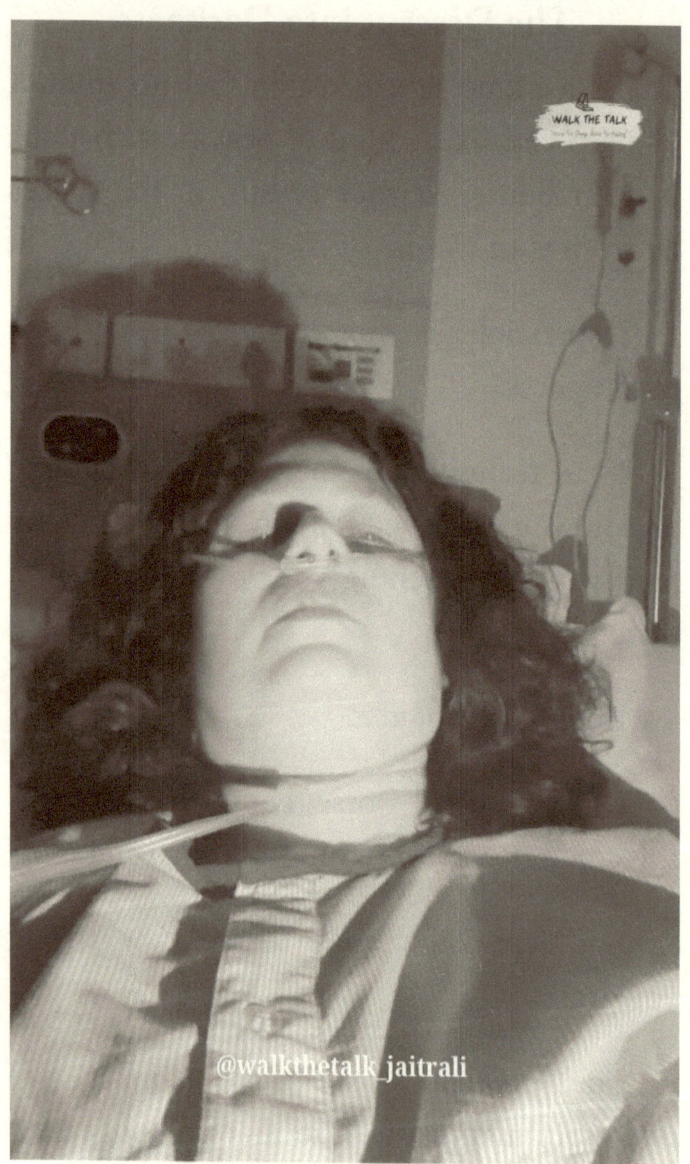
WALK THE TALK
@walkthetalk_jaitrali

like my own, dragged me into a darkness I couldn't escape.

Days blurred into each other. My body moved, but I was no longer present. And then, at some point, I stopped moving altogether.

The breaking point came quietly.

I don't even remember the moment I realised I couldn't keep going—I just remember waking up in a hospital bed, surrounded by white walls and unfamiliar faces, my body filled with chemicals meant to bring me back to life.

Electroconvulsive therapy (ECT). Ketamine infusions. A cocktail of antidepressants that I later called my "gems". Each treatment was meant to fix me, to pull me back from the abyss.

But healing is not just about medicine. It's about finding the will to want to heal.

And in that moment, I wasn't sure if I wanted to anymore. But somewhere deep within me, the rebel still lived. The girl who had walked through fire and survived.

The girl who had been bruised, broken, silenced—and still stood. The girl who refused to be defined by anyone's rules but her own.

She hadn't left.

She had just gone quiet.

Waiting.

And now, she was wide awake.

As I slowly began to reclaim myself—piece by piece, breath by breath—I was confronted by yet another demand: Conformity.

An interfaith marriage brought with it the weight of tradition, the quiet pressure to shift, soften, surrender. To blend into an identity that wasn't mine.

But faith, to me, was never about rules.

It wasn't about rituals passed down like commandments, never to be questioned.

Faith, for me, was personal. Internal. Sacred.

And I had already spent a lifetime being shaped by others' expectations.

So this time, I said no.

Not out of rebellion, but out of clarity.

Not out of disrespect, but out of respect for myself.

I would not trade my identity to make someone else comfortable. I would not silence the fire inside me to keep the peace.

I had fought too hard to be free.

I wasn't about to put myself back in a cage.

And yes, the world labelled me a rebel. Again.

But for the first time in a long time—I felt like myself again.

I had survived trauma.

I had survived betrayal.

I had survived depression.

I had stood on the edge—and I didn't fall.

But life wasn't done with me.

Therapist's Reflection: When Love and Identity Collide

As a psychotherapist, I now recognise the psychological terrain I was navigating at the time:

1. **Depression after trauma isn't weakness—it's a shutdown response.** *When you've carried too much for too long, the body stops to protect what's left.*

2. **Identity crises often emerge after major life transitions.** *Interfaith or intercultural*

relationships can magnify questions of belonging, loyalty, and self-definition.

3. **Healing isn't just about feeling better— it's about remembering who you were before the world told you who to be.** Medication may help stabilize, but the deeper work is in the rediscovery of self.

Journaling Prompts for Readers

If you have ever felt like your body was carrying a weight you couldn't explain, take a moment to reflect on these questions. Write freely, without judgment.

1. What is one part of yourself that you feel you've lost over the years?

2. Have you ever changed or silenced yourself to preserve a relationship? How did that impact you?

3. If you could reclaim one thing about your identity—what would it be, and why?

4. *In what ways can you honour your beliefs and boundaries while still honouring those you love?*

Before the Next Chapter

You can love someone and still choose yourself.

Saying no is not disrespect—it's self-respect.

Belief systems can unite, but they should never erase.

Rebellion isn't about rage—it's about reclaiming.

Take a moment to breathe, feel, and write. This space is yours.

• • •

RECLAIMING MYSELF: THE BATTLE FOR IDENTITY AND INDEPENDENCE

For the longest time, my life had been about survival.

Survival in homes that weren't mine.

Survival in relationships where I had to prove my worth.

Survival in a world that did not recognise invisible pain.

But this time, I wasn't just fighting to survive—I was fighting to reclaim myself.

The first step? Reclaiming my name.

The name I was born with. The name that was taken from me, reshaped by expectations, altered to fit someone else's vision of who I should be. I reclaimed it because it was mine.

And with that decision came the realisation that I needed more.

I needed to become independent again—to prove to

myself that I was still capable, still strong, still in control of my own fate.

I needed a job. A career. A purpose.

What I didn't know was that my career was waiting for me with open arms. The world of Digital Marketing. Where I thrived… Till the inevitable occurred.

When Illness Comes Knocking

An unwanted lifelong companion: Multiple Sclerosis.

An autoimmune disorder. A slow, relentless attack on my body from within.

MS does not negotiate. It does not compromise. It does not care about your plans, your ambitions, or your resilience. It takes. Slowly. Brutally. Until you are forced to face the reality that you are no longer in control.

And if that wasn't enough, in 2010, Crohn's Disease entered the battlefield.

Another autoimmune disorder. Another war.

This time, my doctors raised a red flag—I could no longer work.

But I wasn't ready to hear that.

I defied gravity, pushing through despite my body's protests. I continued my career, refusing to let illness decide my fate.

But corporations are not built for compassion. Not only did I have to let my job go, I lost my ability to walk.

By 2016, I was in a wheelchair.

A loyal companion, I must say. Unlike humans, it never abandoned me.

Multiple Sclerosis is not just a diagnosis—it's a life-altering reality, a silent war waged within one's own body. It is the kind of battle that others cannot see, but you feel in every movement, in every breath, in every uncertain step. One day, your body listens to you, the next, it rebels.

MS is unpredictable. It comes in waves—some days, a dull ache in the background, other days, a full-blown storm. The fatigue is relentless, a bone-deep exhaustion that sleep cannot fix. The numbness, the tingling, the weakness—it's like your body is slowly forgetting how to function. And yet, the world sees nothing. "But you look fine," they say, unaware of the invisible war beneath your skin. That's the hardest part—not just the symptoms, but the loneliness of an illness that exists in the shadows, demanding to be felt but never seen.

Crohn's Disease: The Pain No One Talks About

Crohn's is not just a stomach problem—it is a relentless battle against pain, inflammation and unpredictability. It is waking up with searing abdominal cramps, living in fear of when the next flare-up will strike, never knowing if today will be bearable or a complete shutdown of your body.

It is more than just physical pain; it is the exhaustion that eats away at your energy, the malnutrition that drains your strength, the way your body turns against itself, leaving you vulnerable, raw and endlessly tired. The world does not understand the weight of an illness that forces you to plan your life around restrooms, diet restrictions and sheer willpower. And the worst part? No one sees it. No one understands the toll of a disease that leaves you looking 'normal' while tearing you apart from the inside.

Both MS and Crohn's teach you a painful truth: Invisible illnesses require visible strength. And that strength? It is not just about enduring pain—it is about rising despite it.

The Darkest Question: Now What?

Once again, I slipped into depression. Not because I couldn't work. Not because I was disabled. But because I asked myself, "Now what?"

What was my purpose now? What was left for me when everything I had built had been taken away?

For the first time in my life, I didn't have an answer.

And that terrified me.

From Despair to Purpose

But if life had stripped me of my past, maybe it was time to build something new.

First, I created an autoimmune support group on Facebook—a space to connect, to learn, to understand this invisible devil called autoimmune disease.

But something was missing.

I searched for a therapist who could understand the silent pain of autoimmune disorders—the unpredictable symptoms, the way they erode your identity.

I found no one.

And that's when a thought changed everything:

What if I became the therapist I was looking for?

The Birth of a New Mission

I pursued psychology, not just to heal myself but to understand the depths of the human mind, the connection between body and trauma, the invisible battles that no doctor acknowledges.

And then, Ikigai dawned upon me.

I realigned my life's four pillars:

- Profession – Psychology became my new expertise.

- Vocation – I found purpose in helping others.

- Passion – I loved understanding and healing the human mind.

- Mission – I would raise awareness and validate every autoimmune warrior's silent battle.

So, I built something new. I was lucky, I didn't hunt for clients—they came to me. I didn't charge the ones who couldn't afford therapy—because healing is a right, not a privilege.

And life, once again, was kind.

My work gained recognition, leading me to collaborate with a renowned MS foundation—

writing for their magazine, website and social media.

However, life is relentless. My body betrayed me, yet again.

The worst was at my door.

Paralysis. Not once. But twice.

From Stilettoes to Wheelchair

Still, I refused to stop. Because I had learned something about the inescapable nature of pain.

It demands to be felt.

Pain is the one certainty in life. No matter how much we try to avoid it, escape it, or numb it, it finds us—through loss, through failure, through the unexpected storms that shake our very foundation. It comes in different forms: A heartbreak that shatters your soul, a betrayal that leaves you questioning your worth, dreams slipping through your fingers just when you think they are within reach. And sometimes, it arrives as an unwelcome silence, a void that swallows everything you once knew.

Life is not a straight road; it is a terrain of sharp turns, steep climbs and unpredictable descents. One moment, you are soaring—everything feels aligned, success, love and hope filling your days. And in the next, a single event can send you spiralling, leaving you gasping for air, wondering how quickly everything unravelled. That is the nature of existence—it does not promise fairness, nor does it wait for you to be ready.

But here's the truth: We are not meant to avoid pain. We are meant to endure it, to grow through it, to use it as fuel to keep moving forward.

You will fall, more times than you can count. People will leave. Opportunities will slip away. There will be days when even breathing is a battle. But you are not defined by the pain you endure—you are defined by how you rise from it.

Because even in the worst of times, life still gives us choices.

To let pain break us or to let it shape us.

To let loss define us or to let it teach us.

To close our hearts in fear or to open them despite the risk.

We cannot escape the highs and lows of life. But we can choose to keep walking, to keep hoping, to keep fighting for the life we deserve. Because at the end of the day, pain is not just suffering—it is transformation. And those who learn to embrace it are the ones who come out stronger, wiser and more alive than ever before.

I AM POSSIBLE.

Therapist's Reflection: The Intersection of Illness and Identity

1. *Losing independence is not just physical—it is emotional.*

2. *Chronic illness often leads to a loss of identity, forcing us to rediscover who we are beyond our diagnosis.*

3. *Purpose can be the most powerful medicine.*

Journaling Prompt for Readers

If you have ever felt like your identity was stripped away, take a moment to reflect on these questions. Write freely, without judgment.

1. *What is one part of yourself that you feel you've lost?*

2. *If illness, circumstances, or trauma did not hold you back, what would you pursue?*

3. How can you begin to redefine your purpose today?

Before the Next Chapter

I did not do this alone.

My husband, my children, my immediate family were my unshakable pillars.

Caregivers don't just help—they sacrifice.

They carry the invisible weight of pain, of exhaustion, of watching someone they love fight battles they cannot win for them.

And my gratitude to them is endless.

Because when I had nothing left, they were my reason to keep going.

If there is one thing life has taught me, it is this: You do not get to choose the battles life throws at you. But you do get to choose how you fight them.

I have lived a thousand lives in one.

I have been the child who lost too soon, the girl who had to grow up before her time.

I have been the woman who fought against illness, against betrayal, against a world that tried to shrink her.

And yet—I have risen. Again and again.

Because the fire inside me will always be stronger than the fire that tries to consume me.

I have fought wars I never should have had to fight.

And I have won battles even when the odds were stacked against me.

But the greatest battle of all? The battle to stay soft, to keep believing, to never let life make me bitter.

That is the battle I choose to fight every day.

If you take anything from my story, let it be this: No matter what life throws at you, you have to fight back.

When a door shuts, don't waste time banging on it—look around, because life has already opened another one.

When you feel like everything is falling apart, remember that sometimes, things have to fall apart so they can be rebuilt even stronger.

And when you are at your lowest, when you feel like there is no way forward, remind yourself: This is not the end of your story.

Your Pain is Not the End—It is the Beginning

I have been burned and broken, I have been abandoned and forgotten, I have been told I would never make it.

And yet—I am still here.

And so are you.

Because pain is not the end.

It is the beginning.

It is the place where strength is born.

It is the moment where resilience is built.

It is the fire that forges you into something unbreakable.

And you are unbreakable.

You are not just someone who has suffered.

You are someone who has survived.

Who has fought.

Who has risen.

And you are far from done.

Take a moment to breathe, feel, and write. This space is yours.

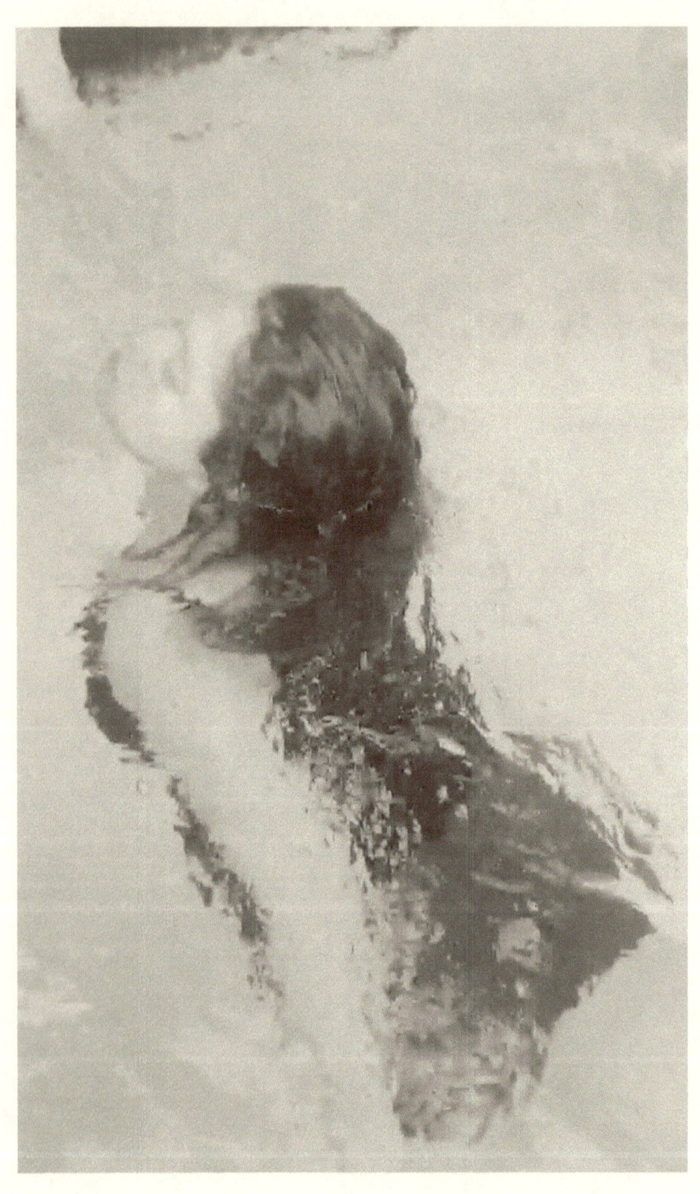

OVERCOMING ADVERSITY

Career highs turned into hospital stays and I suddenly found myself adapting to life in a wheelchair. It felt like my world had shattered. Yet even in these darkest moments, I refused to stay down.

With every setback, I found the strength to rise again, turning my pain into purpose and proving that adversity could be met with an unyielding willpower.

Purpose and Empowerment

My health challenges led me to discover a new calling in the field of mental health. In my toughest days, psychology became my guiding light, a source of understanding and healing that helped me make sense of the turmoil. I realised how much support was missing for people living with chronic autoimmune conditions, not just for patients but for their families as well.

Determined to fill this gap, I pursued psychotherapy and reinvented myself as a mind-health therapist, specialising in helping clients with autoimmune and mental health struggles. Today, I provide a warm, holistic approach to therapy, treating the mind and body as a whole and creating a safe space where individuals can work through their most challenging feelings without shame or guilt.

My own scars have given me a unique insight into pain, allowing me to guide others on how to heal, build resilience and rediscover hope. I truly believe that the human spirit can overcome even the greatest challenges.

A Mission of Empowerment

It is my life's mission to uplift others facing hardships. I have created an online support community,

'Autoimmune – A Silent Killer', to ensure no one battling chronic illness has to feel alone in the dark. As a counsellor, speaker, and now the author of *Scars and Strength*, I provide real-life tools that drive transformation, turning challenges into opportunities through my words and work.

My mission is to help others feel seen, heard, and understood in their pain—because I've walked that path myself—and to build a true community of validation, support, and healing around them.

My message is one of hope, courage, and self-empowerment: With resilience and the right support, every scar can become a story of strength.

There was a time when I begged the universe for an undo button, for a different script, a softer journey. But now, I understand: Every scar, every pain, every moment I thought I wouldn't make it—those were the chapters that shaped me. They forced me to fight, to break, to rebuild, to rise.

WALK THE TALK
@walkthetalk_jaitrali

And I did.

Not in the way fairy tales promise, with grand victories and easy endings. My rise was messy, slow, painful. It was a thousand small choices—choosing to breathe when my body refused, choosing to trust after betrayal, choosing to love when grief made my heart heavy. It was standing up, even when standing felt impossible.

Through it all, I found something I never expected—purpose. What I once saw as weakness became my greatest strength. The silence I once drowned in became my voice. The pain that nearly destroyed me became the very thing that connected me to others who were suffering, waiting for someone to say, *I see you. I understand. You are not alone.*

If my journey has taught me anything, it's this: We are all more resilient than we believe. Our pain does not break us; it reveals us. Strength is not in avoiding scars, but in embracing them, in letting them remind us that we are alive, that we survived, that we are still standing.

So, if you are reading this, carrying your own wounds, wondering if you will ever feel whole again—hear me when I say: You will. You are not alone.

Key Highlights & Roles

- **Digital Media Trailblazer:** 20-year career in digital marketing, including leadership as a CEO and consulting across banking, retail, hospitality, IT and publishing sectors.

- **Award-Winning Marketer:** Featured among the *"Top 10 Powerful Digital Women in India"* and named one of the *"Top 20 International Marketers"* for my contributions to the industry.

- **Autoimmune Advocate:** Founder of the Facebook support group **Autoimmune – A Silent Killer,** creating a community for awareness, empathy and support for those with chronic illness.

- **Mind-Health Expert:** Certified psychotherapist and autoimmune counsellor who integrates mind–body healing practices to help clients overcome mental health challenges and chronic illness hurdles.

- **Author & Speaker:** Author of *Scars and Strength* and a motivational speaker committed to sharing strategies for resilience, personal growth and turning pain into purpose.

My journey from boardroom success to battling invisible illnesses and ultimately to healing others, stands as a powerful testament to human resilience. My voice—both in my counselling practice and in *Scars and Strength*—echoes with hard-earned wisdom and unwavering positivity. In every chapter of my life, I strive to depict how courage, vulnerability and determination can together turn scars into stepping stones toward strength and empowerment

Final Reflection: Stay Tuned for My Second Innings

This book?

It is just the first chapter of my story.

I am not done.

I am just getting started.

So stay tuned for my second innings.

Because I promise you—it will be worth it

Mental Health: No Longer a Stigma, but the Need of the Hour

For generations, mental health was buried under the weight of shame, silence, and stigma. People were taught to "tough it out," to stay strong no matter what, and to never speak of emotional pain. But times are changing. Today, mental health is no longer a taboo subject reserved for only those with clinical diagnoses. It has rightfully become a fundamental part of overall well-being—something every individual should prioritize, regardless of how severe or mild their struggles may seem.

You don't have to be clinically depressed, anxious, or traumatized to seek help. Therapy isn't reserved for "serious" cases. In fact, one of the most empowering things you can do for yourself is ask for support before the pain becomes unbearable.

We don't wait until our teeth are falling out to see a dentist. We go for checkups. We brush. We prevent. The same logic applies to the mind.

Why Therapy Is for Everyone

Sometimes, all we need is an unbiased, non-judgmental, professionally trained listener—someone who isn't part of our immediate circle, who isn't influenced by the past, and who can offer a bird's-eye view of our situation. Friends and family may care, but they often bring their own projections, expectations, and emotions into the conversation.

A therapist, on the other hand, creates a safe space.

A space free of interruptions.

A space where your feelings aren't dismissed as overreactions or labeled "too sensitive."

A space where you're not just heard—but understood.

We all have blind spots. We all experience confusion, stuck, or moments when life just feels too much. And in those moments, reaching out isn't weakness. It's wisdom.

Mental Health isn't Just about Diagnoses

Counselling can help with:

- Gaining clarity during decision-making

- Processing grief or life transitions

- Navigating relationship dynamics

- Managing burnout, self-doubt, or imposter syndrome

- Healing from emotional injuries that didn't seem "big enough" to count

You don't need a label to validate your pain. Your discomfort is valid, your confusion is real, and your healing is worth investing in.

The Shift We All Need

Mental health is no longer just an emergency room. It's also a gym. A mirror. A compass.

It's where we go to strengthen emotional resilience, understand our patterns, and build a relationship with ourselves. The strongest thing you can do is admit when you need perspective—and then take steps to get it.

Let's normalise this.

Let's normalise talking about therapy the way we talk about yoga, fitness, or nutrition. Because mental health is health.

• • •

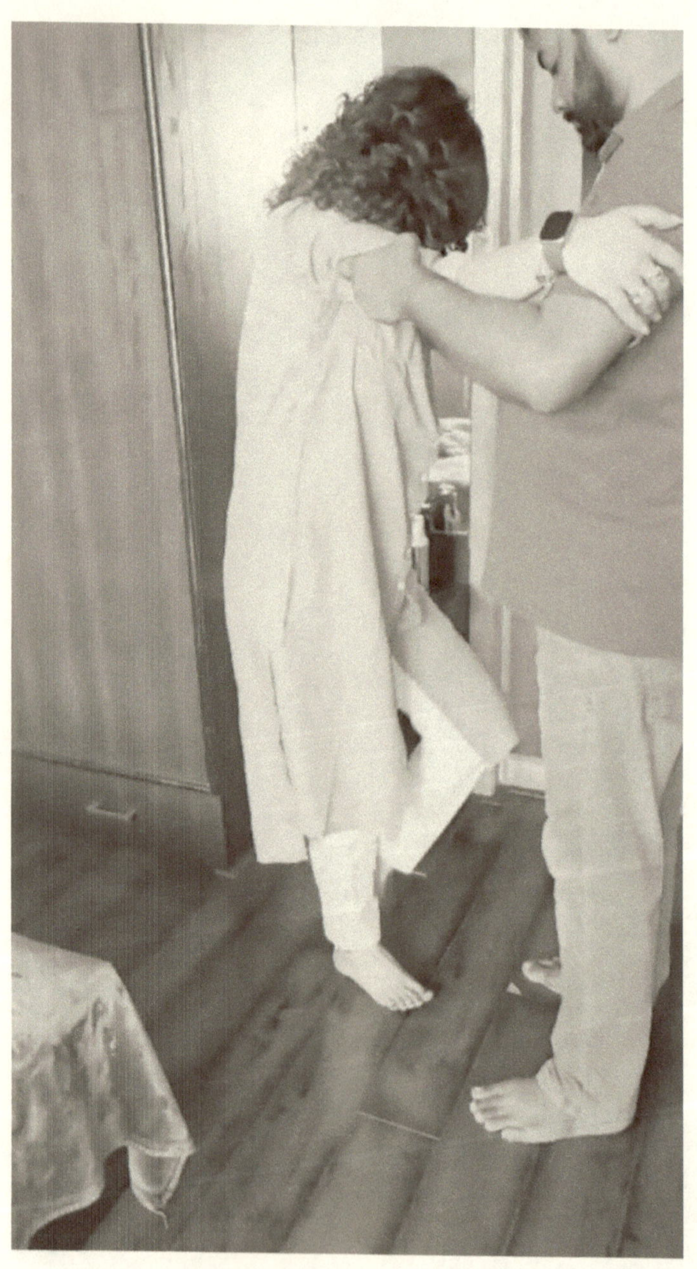

EPILOGUE: THE STRENGTH IN MY SCARS

Scars tell stories. Some are etched on our skin, whispering of battles fought, of fire and survival, of nights spent gasping for breath. Others are carved into our souls, invisible but no less real—proof of heartbreak, betrayal, and the silent wars waged within. My life has been a canvas of both. And yet, standing here now, I am not defined by the wounds—I am defined by the healing.

Though the journey may be long, though the scars may remain, you will one day look back and see what I see now—not just pain, but power. Not just survival, but strength.

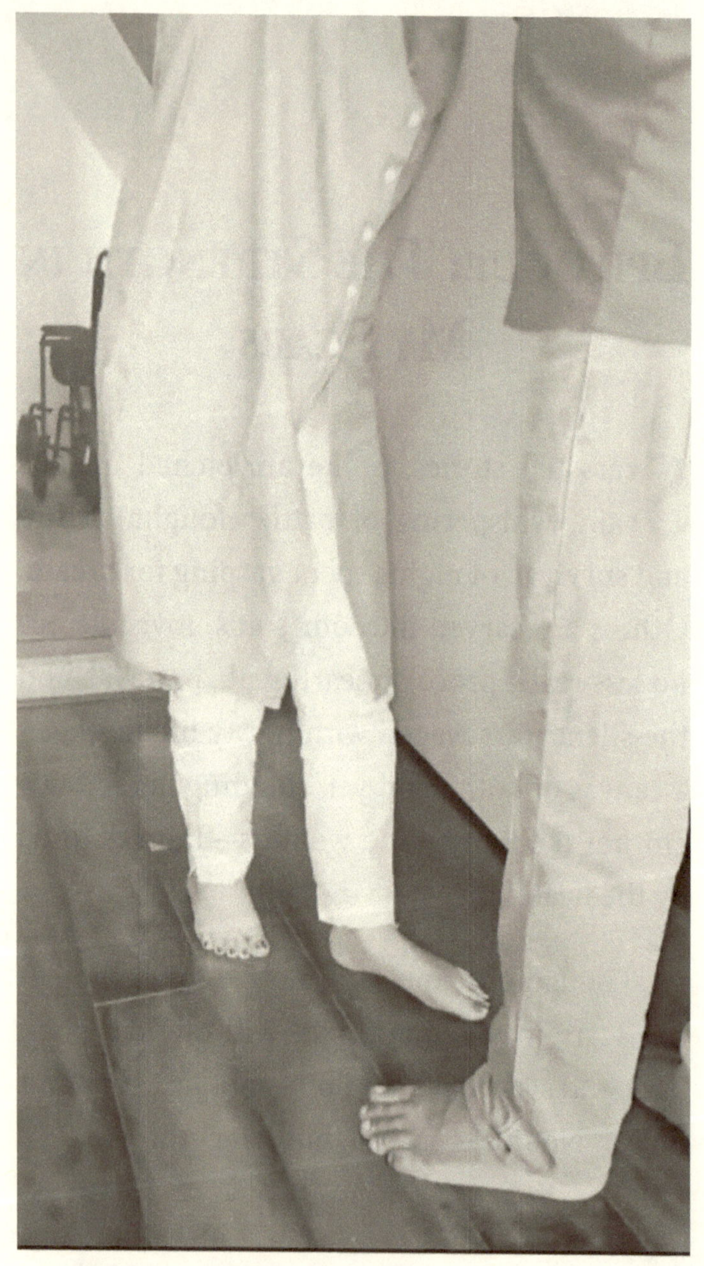

And that? That is the most beautiful kind of victory.

This is not the end. This is only the beginning.

Unveiling Autoimmune Diseases

Autoimmune diseases represent a perplexing and expanding category of medical conditions where the body's immune system, designed to defend against harmful invaders, mistakenly attacks its own healthy tissues. This internal misidentification leads to chronic inflammation, tissue damage and a myriad of health complications that can affect virtually any organ or system within the body.

This is the story of my life. I have lived this. I live this. Daily.

Multiple Sclerosis.

Crohne's disease.

Psychosomatic Asthma.

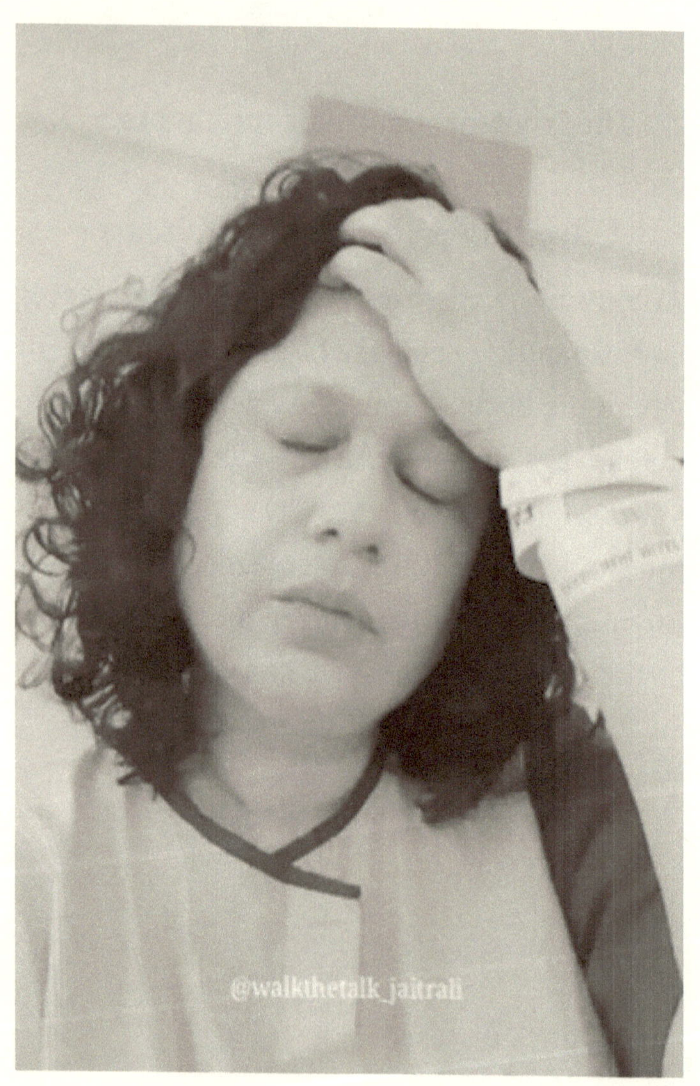
@walkthetalk_jaitrali

What is Multiple Sclerosis?

Multiple Sclerosis (MS) is a chronic, unpredictable disease of the Central Nervous System. It occurs when the body's own immune system, designed to protect us, mistakenly turns against us—targeting the brain, spinal cord and the optic nerves.

MS attacks the myelin—the protective sheath surrounding nerve fibres—much like stripping insulation off electrical wires. Without that crucial coating, communication between the brain and body is disrupted.

Signals are distorted, slowed, or blocked entirely. Over time, the nerves themselves may deteriorate, causing permanent damage.

The effects of MS are far-reaching. They impact physical movement, cognitive function, emotional stability and the overall quality of life.

It is not just a medical condition; it is an unrelenting test of resilience, identity and hope.

What Causes Multiple Sclerosis

The cause of MS remains complex and unclear —genetics, environmental triggers (like viruses), vitamin D deficiency, hormonal shifts and chronic inflammation all play a role.

But there is no single answer. Just a lifetime of questions.

The Real Effects: What MS Feels Like

Living with MS is like carrying one hundred invisible weights on your body and mind.

Fatigue that sleep cannot cure: It feels as if even your bones are surrendering.

Numbness and tingling, like parts of your body have simply disappeared.

Muscle weakness that makes simple tasks feel like climbing mountains.

Memory lapses, cognitive fog: Where words vanish mid-sentence, and names slip away from your own life story.

Vision problems that blur the world, sometimes temporarily, sometimes permanently.

The MS Hug—a misnamed, misunderstood crushing pain that wraps around the torso like a tightening vice.

Loss of bladder or bowel control—a devastating blow to dignity and independence.

Paralysis—temporary for some, heartbreakingly permanent for others.

Depression, anxiety and grief—not only from altered brain chemistry but from mourning the body you once knew.

The cruellest aspect? Most of these symptoms are invisible. The outside world sees a smile; inside, there is a war.

Why It Hurts So Deeply

MS doesn't merely attack the body—it dismantles identity.

One flare-up can steal your independence.

One wrong step can put you in a hospital.

One moment of forgetfulness can spiral into unbearable self-doubt.

Every new symptom is a brutal reminder that control is an illusion.

MS is not just a disease. It is a thief.

It steals time, energy, mobility, dignity, dreams and sometimes even relationships. It forces you to watch, silently, as the world rushes past—while you scream inside a body that has become an unrecognisable battleground.

And yet, despite the pain, despite the theft, despite the invisible wars—we endure.

Not because we chose MS.

But because we refuse to let it erase us.

What is Dr. Crohn's Disease (Inflammatory Bowel Disease aka IBD)

Dr. Crohn's Disease, a form of Inflammatory Bowel Disease (IBD), is a chronic, autoimmune disorder that causes inflammation in the digestive tract.

Named after Dr. Burrill Crohn, who first described it in 1932, this condition can affect any part of the gastrointestinal tract—from the mouth to the anus—but most commonly targets the small intestine and colon.

In Crohn's Disease, the body's immune system mistakenly attacks healthy tissue, triggering persistent inflammation. This inflammation can penetrate deep into the layers of bowel tissue, causing pain, severe diarrhoea, fatigue, weight loss and malnutrition.

The disease is unpredictable, marked by periods of flare-ups and remissions. It is not merely a physical illness; it becomes a constant emotional and psychological challenge—demanding resilience, patience and unyielding strength.

What Causes Dr. Crohn's Disease

The exact cause of Dr. Crohn's Disease remains unclear. Like many autoimmune conditions, it is believed to stem from a combination of factors: Genetic susceptibility, environmental triggers, immune system dysfunction and changes in the gut microbiome.

A family history of IBD significantly increases the risk.

Environmental influences—such as diet, lifestyle, stress and exposure to certain infections—may trigger or exacerbate the disease.

At its core, Crohn's reflects a malfunction of the immune system, where the body cannot distinguish between harmful invaders and its own tissues.

The cruellest part is the unpredictability—flare-ups can strike without warning, and periods of remission can be fleeting, leaving individuals in a constant state of uncertainty and vigilance.

What Living with Dr. Crohn's Disease Feels Like

Living with Dr. Crohn's Disease is like being trapped in a body that rebels without reason. It is an exhausting, isolating experience that infiltrates every aspect of daily life.

Severe abdominal pain and cramping: Sharp, relentless and often without warning.

Chronic diarrhoea: With an urgency and frequency that strip away freedom and dignity.

Debilitating fatigue: A level of exhaustion that no amount of rest can erase.

Nausea and vomiting: Where food becomes the enemy, robbing both strength and joy.

Unintentional weight loss and malnutrition: As the body struggles to absorb essential nutrients.

Joint pain and inflammation: Pain that extends beyond the gut, affecting mobility and quality of life.

Skin rashes, eye inflammation, and liver disorders: Silent reminders that Crohn's does not stay confined to the digestive system.

Fistulas and abscesses: Painful, sometimes life-threatening complications arising from chronic inflammation.

And yet, most of this battle is invisible.

On the outside, you may look healthy. Inside, a relentless war wages—unseen, misunderstood and exhausting.

Why it Hurts So Deeply

Dr. Crohn's Disease doesn't just assault the digestive system—it assaults the essence of daily life.

Every meal becomes a gamble.

Every outing is planned around the nearest restroom.

Every plan is laced with a silent "what if?"

It is a thief that steals energy, spontaneity and sometimes even the desire to socialise or dream. It traps you in cycles of hope and despair—of wishing for normalcy while preparing for the next invisible battle.

Perhaps the deepest wound is the loss of trust in your own body. To live with Dr. Crohn's Disease is to live with a betrayal from within, battling not just physical symptoms but the emotional erosion of confidence, independence and hope.

And yet, through the pain, many of us rise— not because we chose this war, but because survival demands a courage most will never have to understand.

What is a Psychosomatic Attack

A Psychosomatic Attack is a physical crisis triggered by the body's emotional and psychological distress.

Unlike traditional illnesses, where pathogens are the enemy, psychosomatic attacks emerge from within. The body responds to unresolved emotions, stress and anxiety.

One of the most terrifying manifestations is psychosomatic shortness of breath—where the lungs themselves are healthy, but the brain signals the body into a state of panic, constriction and suffocation.

There is no infection.

There is no obstruction.

Yet the body reacts as if it is under siege.

What makes psychosomatic attacks so cruel is that they are very real—felt with the same intensity as physical diseases—but they rarely leave visible traces on medical tests. As they exist in the grey space between mind and body, they are often misunderstood, minimised, or dismissed.

Treatment isn't found in traditional medication alone.

Healing lies in addressing the emotional wounds that have woven themselves into the body's fabric.

What Causes a Psychosomatic Attack

Psychosomatic attacks are born from the complex interaction between the mind, the body and emotions. When emotional pain—fear, grief, anger, or trauma—is suppressed or unresolved, the body seeks release. But instead of tears or words, the pain manifests physically.

Triggers for Psychosomatic Attacks Include:

Prolonged emotional stress

Anxiety disorders

Past traumas

Chronic internalised emotions like guilt, shame, or fear

Unresolved grief or loss

The nervous system, overwhelmed by hidden emotional chaos, sends distress signals that tighten the chest, restrict breathing and flood the body with sensations of danger. The brain and body fall into a loop of perceived threat—creating very real physical suffering without a clear external cause.

Unlike traditional illnesses, there is no medication that can "cure" a psychosomatic attack. Healing requires emotional processing, nervous system regulation, therapy, mindfulness and deep inner work.

The Real Effects: What a Psychosomatic Attack Feels Like

Living with psychosomatic attacks is akin to being imprisoned by your own body's alarms, without knowing where the fire is.

Shortness of breath: A terrifying sensation of not getting enough air, even when nothing is blocking the lungs.

Tightness in the chest: As if an invisible band is tightening around your ribs, making each breath a desperate effort.

Shallow breathing: Where only the upper part of the lungs fills, leaving the body starved for oxygen.

Panic or dread: Even when there is no visible threat, the heart races, the hands shake and the mind spirals.

Dizziness and faintness: Oxygen deprivation tricks the brain into believing collapse is imminent.

Fatigue: Profound exhaustion from the body's endless cycles of tension and struggle to survive an invisible enemy.

Numbness and tingling: Especially in the fingers, toes, or around the mouth, as Carbon Dioxide builds up from improper breathing.

Tears without warning: A release valve for emotions the body cannot otherwise express.

Even when the attack passes, the fear of it returning haunts every moment. Every short breath, every racing heartbeat, becomes a potential trigger for another episode.

Why It Hurts So Deeply

A psychosomatic attack doesn't just steal your breath—it steals your sense of safety within yourself.

It creates a terrifying rift between mind and body—where you can no longer trust your own lungs, your own heartbeat, your own instincts. It leaves you feeling isolated, invalidated, because the suffering is real—but the medical reports may show "nothing wrong".

It is a thief that robs not just the ability to breathe freely, but the freedom to live without fear.

It traps you inside your own body, convincing you that every moment of calm is fragile, temporary and could shatter without warning.

The world may continue, unaware. But inside, you are fighting for every breath—sometimes without understanding why. And that is a pain few can comprehend unless they have lived it.

Understanding Autoimmune Diseases

In a properly functioning immune system, foreign pathogens such as bacteria and viruses are identified and neutralised to protect the body. However, in autoimmune diseases, this defence mechanism goes awry. The immune system loses its ability to distinguish between self and non-self, resulting in an assault on the body's own cells. This misguided attack can lead to a wide range of symptoms, depending on the specific tissues or organs involved.

Common Features Across Autoimmune Conditions

Despite the diversity among autoimmune diseases, several commonalities exist:

- **Inflammation:** A hallmark of autoimmune responses, leading to redness, heat, pain and swelling in affected areas.

- **Fatigue:** Persistent tiredness is frequently reported, significantly impacting daily activities and quality of life.

- **Flares and Remissions:** Many autoimmune diseases are characterised by periods of intensified symptoms (flares) followed by intervals of relative relief (remissions).

Global Prevalence and Rising Trends

Autoimmune diseases have become a significant global health concern:

- **Prevalence:** Recent studies indicate that approximately one in ten individuals worldwide is affected by an autoimmune disorder.

- **Increasing Incidence:** The prevalence and incidence of autoimmune diseases are rising globally, with yearly increases estimated at 12.5% and 19.1%, respectively.

Causes and Contributing Factors

The exact causes of autoimmune diseases remain elusive, but several factors are believed to contribute:

- **Genetic Predisposition:** A family history of autoimmune diseases can increase susceptibility.

- **Environmental Triggers:** Infections, exposure to certain chemicals, and dietary components may initiate or exacerbate autoimmune responses.

- **Lifestyle Factors:** Stress, lack of physical activity, and poor diet are associated with increased risk.

Treatment and Management

While cures for autoimmune diseases are rare, various treatments aim to manage symptoms and modulate the immune response:

- **Medication:** Nonsteroidal anti-inflammatory drugs (NSAIDs) alleviate pain and inflammation; immunosuppressants reduce immune system activity.

- **Lifestyle Modifications:** Balanced nutrition, regular exercise and stress management can help control symptoms and improve overall well-being.

- **Biologic Therapies:** Target specific components of the immune system to reduce inflammation and prevent tissue damage.

The Need for Widespread Awareness

Awareness of autoimmune diseases is crucial for several reasons:

- **Early Detection:** Recognising symptoms promptly can lead to earlier diagnosis and intervention, potentially mitigating disease progression.

- **Broad Susceptibility:** Autoimmune diseases can affect anyone, regardless of age, gender, or background. Universal awareness fosters a more supportive and understanding society.

- **Educational Outreach:** Informing the general public, including corporate entities, about autoimmune diseases can lead to more accommodating workplaces and policies. Discrimination against individuals with these conditions should be addressed, and in some jurisdictions, may be considered a punishable offense.

Encouraging Treatment and Reducing Stigma

Seeking treatment is vital for managing autoimmune diseases effectively. Disclosure of one's condition can facilitate access to necessary accommodations and support systems. Reducing stigma associated with these diseases encourages individuals to pursue medical care without fear of judgment.

Economic Considerations and Accessibility

The financial burden of managing autoimmune diseases can be substantial. Efforts should be made to reduce treatment costs and ensure affordability, recognizing that these diseases do not discriminate based on caste, creed, or socioeconomic status. Equitable access to healthcare resources is essential for all affected individuals.

In a nutshell

Autoimmune diseases present a significant and escalating global health challenge, affecting approximately one in 10 individuals worldwide. The annual increase in incidence and prevalence underscores the urgency for heightened awareness, early detection and comprehensive management strategies.

Raising awareness is not solely the responsibility of those directly affected or their caregivers; it is a societal imperative. Autoimmune diseases do not discriminate based on age, gender, or socioeconomic status, making it essential for everyone to be informed. Early recognition of symptoms can lead to prompt medical attention, improving outcomes and quality of life.

Educational initiatives should extend to corporate environments to foster supportive workplaces. Understanding and accommodating employees with autoimmune conditions not only promote inclusivity but also enhance productivity and morale. Discrimination against individuals with these diseases is not only unethical but may also be subject to legal consequences.

Financial accessibility to treatments remains a critical concern. The rising prevalence of autoimmune diseases has led to increased healthcare expenditures, with global spending reaching significant figures in recent years. Efforts must be directed toward reducing costs and ensuring that effective therapies are affordable for all, irrespective of socioeconomic standing.

In conclusion, a collective effort encompassing public education, supportive workplace policies, and equitable healthcare access is vital in addressing the challenges posed by autoimmune diseases. By fostering a well-informed and compassionate society, we can improve the lives of those affected and mitigate the broader impact of these pervasive conditions.

Why Therapy Matters—Not Just for Patients, But for Caregivers Too

Living with an autoimmune disease is not just a physical experience—it's deeply emotional and psychological. Chronic illness affects the mind as much as it does the body. But in this silent suffering, we often forget another group of warriors walking a parallel path: the caregivers.

For Patients: Holding Space for the Self

Therapy offers a safe space for patients to process the grief of what was lost—health, independence, identity, sometimes even dreams. Autoimmune diseases can be unpredictable and invisible to the outside world, leading to isolation, anxiety and depression.

Patients often face:

- **Emotional exhaustion** from managing flares and the rollercoaster of symptoms.

- **Body betrayal**—feeling like their own body has turned against them.

- **Social withdrawal** due to fatigue, stigma, or lack of understanding.

- **Fear of being a burden**, which can lead to guilt and shame.

Therapy helps patients:

- Reclaim their voice and identity.

- Build resilience and coping strategies.

- Navigate relationships with partners, children, friends, and employers.

- Understand the connection between stress, trauma, and physical symptoms.

For Caregivers: The Invisible Load

Caregivers are the silent anchors, but in holding someone else together, they often begin to unravel themselves. The emotional labour they carry is immense—and rarely acknowledged.

woapodcast_ kamlksh_shetty and walkthetalkwithme   0:40
ON AIR
@woapodcast
Who's on air

They face:

- **Burnout** from constant vigilance and responsibility.

- **Resentment and guilt**, often in the same breath.

- **Fear of the unknown**, watching someone they love suffer and being helpless to stop it.

- **Neglected self-care**, putting the patient's needs above their own, always.

Therapy helps caregivers:

- Validate their own emotions, without judgment.

- Set healthy boundaries while remaining compassionate.

- Process grief, anger, and exhaustion in a safe, non-blaming environment.

- Learn to support without losing themselves.

Why is This Important

Both patients and caregivers are living with trauma—one embodied, the other absorbed. Ignoring either side creates a gap in healing. The relationship between the patient and caregiver can thrive or break under pressure. Therapy strengthens the bond by giving both parties the tools to understand each other's journeys and meet in empathy rather than frustration.

In truth, no one emerges from chronic illness untouched.

Therapy isn't a luxury—it's a lifeline. For the one in pain, and the one who watches it. For the one who fights daily battles inside their body, and the one who stands beside them, fighting in silence.

The Main Underlying Causes:

1. **Genetic Susceptibility**
   Some individuals are born with genes that make them more vulnerable to developing autoimmune conditions. These often involve **HLA (Human Leukocyte Antigen)** markers, which influence how the immune system responds to internal and external threats.

2. **Environmental Triggers**
   Environmental exposures can play a significant role in activating autoimmune responses, especially in genetically predisposed individuals:

   - **Infections** (e.g., Epstein-Barr virus)

   - **Toxins and chemicals** (such as BPA, mercury, and pesticides)

   - **Dietary factors** (processed foods, gluten, dairy in sensitive individuals)

   - **Gut imbalances** (leaky gut, dysbiosis)

3. **Hormonal Influences**

Hormones significantly affect immune function:

- **Estrogen** can enhance immune system activity, which may explain why approximately **80% of autoimmune patients are women**.

- **Testosterone** tends to suppress immune responses, which might offer men some degree of protection—though it doesn't eliminate the risk.

4. **Chronic Stress and Psychological Trauma**

Long-term stress and unresolved trauma can dysregulate the **HPA axis (hypothalamic-pituitary-adrenal axis)**. This disruption affects how the body manages inflammation and immune responses, often increasing vulnerability to autoimmune disorders.

5. **Molecular Mimicry**

   This occurs when the immune system mistakes the body's own tissues for foreign invaders because they share similar molecular structures. It often follows an infection, where the immune response "mimics" the attack, but ends up targeting healthy tissues instead.

6. **Loss of Immune Tolerance**

   In healthy individuals, the immune system can differentiate between "self" and "non-self." In autoimmune conditions, this tolerance is lost, leading the immune system to attack the body's own cells and organs, mistaking them for threats.

Key Takeaway

Autoimmune conditions aren't caused by just one thing. They result from a convergence of factors: a genetic predisposition, environmental triggers, chronic stress, hormonal and gut imbalances, and often unresolved emotional trauma. It's not about a single moment—but the cumulative impact of many.

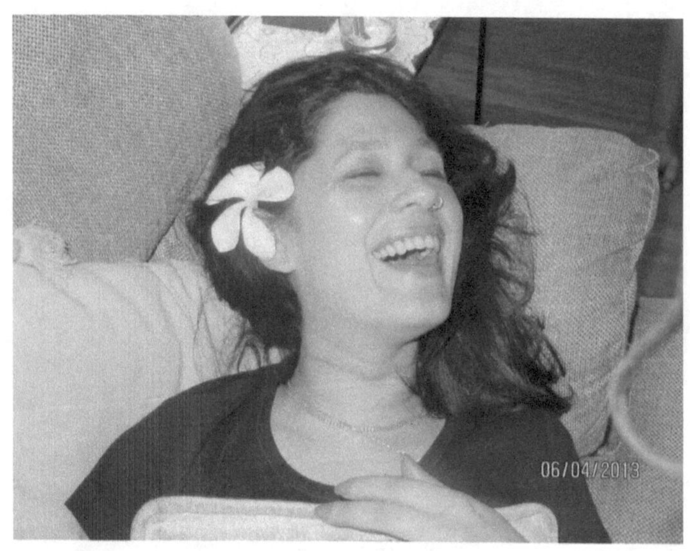

06/04/2013

Author's Bio

About the Author: Jaitrali Jhanjharya

Background and Early Career

Jaitrali Jhanjharya is a **psychotherapist, author, and former digital marketing executive** whose life journey exemplifies resilience and transformation. For nearly two decades, she made her mark in the digital media industry – rising to top leadership roles and even serving as a CEO in the marketing realm . During this period, Jaitrali earned recognition as one of the *"Top 10 Powerful Digital Women in India"* and a *"Top 20 International Marketer,"* reflecting her pioneering contributions to the field . She brought a wealth of expertise in strategic planning, creative development, and interactive media, **unlocking the full potential of every project** she undertook. This successful early career established her as a dynamic and visionary leader in the digital age and now a mission she has given herself to raise awareness, not only about autoimmune but also mental health.

Its not a stigma, it's a brave step you take when you agree to therapy but a bold step of not being a victim but a warrior facing the adversities, and seeking help to conquer the world.

SYNOPSIS

Scars and Strength

"Some battles are fought in silence. Some scars are unseen. But every wound tells a story."

From losing her father at a young age to navigating a life of instability, betrayal and chronic illness, Jaitrali has lived through pain that would break most. Yet, she refused to be defined by it.

In *Scars and Strength*, she shares her raw, unfiltered journey—a testament to resilience, survival, and the relentless pursuit of purpose.

This book is not just a memoir. It's a guide for every soul who has ever felt unseen, unheard, or underestimated.

Through heartbreak, healing, and an unshakable will to rise, Jaitrali proves that scars are not a sign of weakness—they are proof that we survived.

"If life knocks you down, stand up stronger. If doors close, find the ones that are open. Because your story isn't over yet."

Stay tuned for her second innings. It will be worth it.

Let's Keep in Touch

This book is just the beginning of our conversation. If something you read touched your heart, I'd be honored to hear from you.

✉ Write to me at:

walkthetalkjaitrali@gmail.com

www.ingramcontent.com/pod-product-compliance
Lightning Source LLC
Chambersburg PA
CBHW060532160726
47991CB00001B/282